Retirement Asset Mortgage Qualification

How to Use 401(k), IRA, and Investment Accounts for Asset-Based Mortgage Approval

By Joseph G. Correa

Licensed Mortgage Broker, Finibi Mortgage

Copyright & Legal Notice

Published by Live Stronger Faster

The information provided in this book is for educational and informational purposes only and does not constitute financial, legal, tax, or investment advice. The author and publisher make no representations or warranties regarding the accuracy, completeness, or applicability of the content. Readers are encouraged to consult with licensed professionals, including mortgage lenders, financial advisors, tax professionals, and attorneys, before making any financial decisions.

The strategies and examples discussed in this book are illustrative in nature and may not be suitable for all individuals or situations. Results may vary based on market

First Edition, 2026

Table of Contents

Foreword

The traditional mortgage system was built on one core assumption: that income is the primary indicator of a borrower's ability to repay a loan. For decades, lenders have relied heavily on W-2 wages, tax returns, and employment stability to determine eligibility. But this model fails to capture a large and growing segment of financially strong individuals—those who have accumulated substantial wealth but may not have consistent or documentable income. Retirees, early investors, business owners, and financially independent individuals often find themselves in a paradox: they have more than enough assets to support a mortgage, yet they struggle to qualify under outdated underwriting standards. This book exists to solve that problem.

Retirement asset mortgage qualification represents a fundamental shift in how lenders evaluate financial strength. Instead of focusing on what you earn each month, this strategy focuses on what you already own. It recognizes that a borrower with significant retirement savings—whether in a 401(k), IRA, or other investment account—has the capacity to sustain mortgage payments over time, even without traditional income streams. In many ways, this approach aligns more closely with real financial reality. After all, wealth is not just about income; it is about resources, liquidity, and long-term stability.

As more individuals move away from traditional employment models and toward asset-driven lifestyles, the importance of understanding retirement asset-based mortgage qualification continues to grow. Today, people are retiring earlier, building passive income streams, and structuring their finances in ways that do not always produce predictable monthly income. At the same time, they may hold hundreds of thousands—or even millions—of dollars in retirement accounts. These funds, when properly structured and documented, can be used to qualify for mortgage financing in a way that traditional underwriting often overlooks.

This book is designed to bridge the gap between wealth and access. It will show you how to translate retirement assets into qualifying income, how lenders calculate asset depletion, and how to position your financial profile to meet underwriting guidelines. You will learn how different types of retirement accounts are treated, how penalties and access restrictions are considered, and how to structure your assets to maximize your borrowing power. More importantly, you will gain a clear understanding of how to think like an underwriter—so you can anticipate challenges, avoid common mistakes, and secure approval with confidence. One of the most important concepts you will learn is that not all assets are treated equally. A 401(k) account, for example, may be subject to employer restrictions or early withdrawal penalties, while an IRA may offer more flexibility depending on your age and structure. Brokerage accounts, annuities, and other investment vehicles each carry their own rules, risk profiles, and accessibility considerations. Lenders evaluate these factors carefully, applying specific formulas to determine how much of your assets can realistically be used to support a mortgage. Understanding these nuances is the key to unlocking the full potential of your financial portfolio.

Another critical principle is the concept of asset depletion. This method allows lenders to convert your total assets into a hypothetical income stream over a defined period—often 10, 20, or 30 years. By dividing your assets across this timeframe, lenders create a consistent monthly income figure that can be used for qualification purposes. This approach eliminates the need for traditional income documentation and instead focuses on long-term financial sustainability. However, the exact calculation can vary depending on the lender, loan program, and risk tolerance, which is why strategic positioning becomes so important.

In addition to the technical aspects of qualification, this book will also address the mindset shift required to succeed in asset-based lending. Many borrowers approach the mortgage process with assumptions rooted in traditional income-based models. They may believe they need to withdraw funds, generate taxable income, or restructure their finances unnecessarily. In reality, the goal is often the opposite: to preserve your assets while using them strategically to qualify. By understanding how lenders view your financial profile, you can make informed decisions that protect your wealth while achieving your real estate goals.

This book is not just for retirees in the traditional sense. It is for anyone who has built significant assets and wants to leverage them effectively. Whether you are transitioning out of a career, living off investments, or simply prefer not to rely on conventional income documentation, the strategies outlined here will give you a powerful advantage. You will learn how to qualify for a primary residence, refinance an existing property, or even expand into investment real estate—all without the limitations of traditional underwriting.

As you move through this book, you will begin to see that asset-based mortgage qualification is not a loophole or a workaround. It is a legitimate, structured, and increasingly mainstream approach to lending. Financial institutions are recognizing that wealth-based borrowers represent a low-risk, high-quality segment of the market. By aligning their underwriting models with this reality, they are creating opportunities for borrowers who were previously underserved. This shift is not temporary; it is part of a broader evolution in how financial strength is defined.

You will also discover that preparation is everything. The difference between approval and denial often comes down to how your assets are documented, structured, and presented. Small details—such as how accounts are titled, how funds are seasoned, or how distributions are handled—can have a significant impact on your eligibility. Throughout this book, you will learn how to optimize these factors, ensuring that your financial profile is positioned in the strongest possible way before you ever submit an application.

Ultimately, this book is about empowerment. It is about giving you the knowledge and tools to take control of your financing options, regardless of your income situation. It is about breaking free from outdated constraints and leveraging your assets in a way that supports your long-term goals. Whether you are purchasing your dream home, restructuring your existing debt, or building a real estate portfolio, the strategies you learn here will open doors that traditional lending models often keep closed.

The world of mortgage lending is changing, and those who

understand how to navigate asset-based qualification will have a distinct advantage. As you begin this journey, keep in mind that your assets are not just numbers on a statement—they are a powerful foundation for opportunity. When used correctly, they can provide access, flexibility, and financial freedom in ways that traditional income never could. This book will show you how to harness that power and turn it into real, tangible results.

Welcome to a new way of qualifying for real estate—one where your wealth works for you, your strategy defines your success, and your future is no longer limited by how you earn, but expanded by what you have built.

Chapter 1

Understanding Retirement Assets as Qualifying Income

The concept of using retirement assets to qualify for a mortgage represents one of the most important shifts in modern lending. For decades, lenders have been conditioned to evaluate borrowers based on active income—employment wages, self-employment earnings, or verifiable business income. However, this framework overlooks a critical truth: many individuals accumulate wealth over time and eventually transition into a phase of life where their income decreases or becomes less predictable, even as their financial strength increases. Retirement accounts such as 401(k)s, IRAs, and other investment portfolios are often substantial, yet they are frequently misunderstood or underutilized in the mortgage qualification process. This chapter introduces the foundational principles that allow these assets to be transformed into qualifying income, enabling borrowers to access real estate financing without relying on traditional income streams.

Retirement assets are fundamentally different from liquid cash or standard investment accounts because they are typically designed for long-term growth and may carry restrictions on access. These restrictions often include penalties for early withdrawal, required minimum distributions at certain ages, and tax implications that vary depending on the account type. Despite these limitations, lenders recognize that retirement assets still represent real financial strength. The key is determining how much of those assets can reasonably be used to support mortgage payments over time. This is where the concept of asset-based qualification becomes essential.

At its core, retirement asset qualification involves converting a borrower's total asset base into a hypothetical income stream. Instead of asking, "How much do you earn each month?" lenders ask, "If these assets were used over time, how much income could they generate?" This approach aligns more closely with how retirees actually live. Most retirees do not rely on a paycheck; they rely on a combination of withdrawals, investment growth, and strategic financial planning. By modeling this behavior, lenders can create a realistic picture of a borrower's ability to repay a loan.

One of the primary methods used in this process is asset depletion. Asset depletion allows lenders to spread a borrower's assets over a specific number of months, effectively creating a monthly income figure. For example, if a borrower has $1,000,000 in retirement assets, a lender may divide that amount over 360 months (30 years), resulting in a calculated monthly income. This figure can then be used in the same way as traditional income when evaluating debt-to-income ratios. However, the process is not always this straightforward. Lenders may apply discounts to account for market volatility, liquidity concerns, and access restrictions. Understanding how these adjustments work is critical to maximizing your qualifying income.

Different types of retirement accounts are treated differently in the underwriting process. A 401(k), for instance, may be partially discounted if the borrower is not yet of retirement age, due to potential penalties for early withdrawal. Traditional IRAs and Roth IRAs each have their own tax implications, which can affect how distributions are calculated. Some lenders may require proof that the borrower has the ability to access these funds without significant hardship, while others may focus more on the overall asset value and long-term sustainability. The nuances of each account type can significantly impact the final qualifying income figure, making it essential to understand how your specific assets will be evaluated.

Another important factor is the borrower's age and stage of life. A borrower who is already retired and taking regular distributions from their retirement accounts may have an easier time qualifying, as their income stream is already established. In contrast, a younger borrower with substantial retirement savings but no current distributions may need to rely more heavily on asset depletion calculations. In some cases, lenders may require a combination of both approaches, using actual distributions where available and supplementing them with asset-based calculations.

It is also important to consider the role of investment performance. Retirement accounts are often invested in stocks, bonds, mutual funds, or other assets that can fluctuate in value. Lenders are aware of this volatility and may apply conservative assumptions when calculating qualifying income. For example, they may only consider a percentage of the total account value or use historical averages to estimate sustainable withdrawals. This conservative approach is designed to ensure that the borrower can continue to make payments even if market conditions change.

Documentation plays a critical role in retirement asset qualification. Lenders typically require detailed account statements, evidence of ownership, and sometimes a history of contributions or distributions. The more organized and transparent your financial records are, the smoother the underwriting process will be. In many cases, borrowers who understand how to present their assets effectively can significantly improve their chances of approval. This includes consolidating accounts where appropriate, ensuring funds are properly seasoned, and clearly demonstrating access to the assets being used for qualification.

Another key consideration is liquidity. While retirement accounts represent wealth, not all of that wealth is immediately accessible. Lenders must determine how quickly and easily the borrower can convert these assets into cash if needed. Accounts with high liquidity, such as brokerage accounts, may be treated more favorably than those with strict withdrawal limitations. However, even less liquid accounts can still be used effectively if they are properly structured and documented.

The strategic use of retirement assets also involves understanding how to balance qualification with long-term financial health. Just because you can use your assets to qualify for a larger loan does not mean you should. Borrowers must consider their overall financial goals, including preserving capital, managing risk, and maintaining flexibility. The goal is not simply to obtain approval, but to do so in a way that supports long-term stability and growth.

As you begin to understand the principles outlined in this chapter, you will start to see that retirement asset qualification is both an art and a science. It requires a clear understanding of lender guidelines, combined with strategic financial planning. By mastering these concepts, you can position yourself as a strong borrower, regardless of your income situation. This knowledge will serve as the foundation for the more advanced strategies covered in the chapters ahead.

Real-Life Math Example: Translating Retirement Assets into Qualifying Income

Consider a borrower named Michael, who is 62 years old and recently retired from a long career in corporate management. Michael does not have traditional employment income, but he has accumulated significant retirement savings over the years. His financial profile includes $800,000 in a traditional IRA, $200,000 in a Roth IRA, and $150,000 in a brokerage account. In total, Michael has $1,150,000 in assets that could potentially be used for mortgage qualification.

Michael wants to purchase a home and needs to demonstrate sufficient income to qualify for a mortgage. Since he does not have a paycheck, the lender decides to use an asset depletion method to calculate his qualifying income. The first step is determining which assets are eligible and how they will be adjusted. The lender reviews Michael's accounts and applies a conservative approach. The traditional IRA is discounted by 30% to account for taxes and potential penalties, resulting in an adjusted value of $560,000. The Roth IRA, being tax-free upon withdrawal, is discounted by only 10%, resulting in

$180,000. The brokerage account, which is fully liquid, is used at 100% of its value, contributing $150,000. After these adjustments, Michael's total usable assets equal $890,000. The lender then divides this amount over a 30-year term, or 360 months, to calculate a monthly income. When $890,000 is divided by 360, the result is approximately $2,472 per month. This figure becomes Michael's qualifying income for mortgage purposes.

However, the lender does not stop there. Michael also receives Social Security benefits of $1,800 per month. This income is added to the asset-based income, bringing his total qualifying income to $4,272 per month. The lender then evaluates Michael's existing debts, which include a car payment of $400 per month and minimal credit card obligations totaling $100 per month. His total monthly debt is $500.

To determine Michael's eligibility, the lender calculates his debt-to-income ratio. With $500 in monthly debt and $4,272 in qualifying income, his debt-to-income ratio is approximately 11.7%, which is well within acceptable limits. This strong ratio allows Michael to qualify for a mortgage comfortably, despite having no traditional employment income.

Now consider how small changes could impact the outcome. If Michael had not structured his accounts properly or if the lender applied more aggressive discounts, his qualifying income could be significantly lower. For example, if the traditional IRA were discounted by 50% instead of 30%, his adjusted assets would decrease substantially, reducing his monthly income and potentially affecting his approval.

This example illustrates the importance of understanding how retirement assets are evaluated and how strategic planning can influence the final result. By positioning his assets effectively and working with a lender who understands asset-based qualification, Michael is able to achieve his goal of homeownership without relying on traditional income.

Through this process, it becomes clear that retirement assets are not just a safety net for the future—they are a powerful tool for accessing opportunities in the present. When used correctly, they can open doors that might otherwise remain closed, providing flexibility, security, and financial independence in the mortgage process.

Chapter 2

How Lenders Evaluate Retirement Accounts for Mortgage Qualification

As borrowers move deeper into the world of asset-based mortgage qualification, it becomes essential to understand not just that retirement assets can be used, but how lenders actually evaluate those assets behind the scenes. The difference between approval and denial often comes down to how an underwriter interprets your accounts, applies adjustments, and determines what portion of your wealth is truly usable for mortgage qualification. This chapter focuses on the lender's perspective, breaking down the exact thought process, guidelines, and risk considerations that shape how retirement assets are converted into qualifying income.

When a lender reviews a file that relies on retirement assets instead of traditional income, the first question they ask is not how much the borrower has, but how accessible those funds are. Accessibility is one of the most critical factors in asset-based underwriting. Retirement accounts, unlike checking or savings accounts, are governed by rules that may limit when and how funds can be withdrawn. These rules vary depending on the type of account, the borrower's age, and the structure of the account itself. For example, a borrower under the age of 59½ may face early withdrawal penalties on certain retirement accounts, which reduces the effective value of those funds in the eyes of the lender.

This leads to the next major component of evaluation: discounting. Lenders rarely use the full face value of a retirement account when calculating qualifying income. Instead, they apply a discount to account for taxes, penalties, and market risk. The size of this discount can vary depending on the loan program and the lender's internal guidelines, but it is common to see adjustments ranging from 10% to 50%. For instance, a traditional IRA may be discounted more heavily than a Roth IRA because withdrawals from a traditional IRA are taxable, whereas Roth IRA distributions are generally tax-free. This difference directly impacts how much of the asset can be considered usable.

Another layer of evaluation involves determining whether the borrower is currently drawing income from their retirement accounts. If a borrower is already taking regular distributions, lenders may treat those distributions as income, provided they can be documented and are expected to continue. This approach simplifies the process because it aligns with traditional income verification methods. However, if the borrower is not taking distributions, the lender must rely on asset depletion or similar calculations to create a hypothetical income stream. This is where underwriting becomes more complex and requires careful analysis.

The time horizon used in asset depletion calculations is another critical factor. Lenders typically spread the usable assets over a fixed number of months, such as 240 months (20 years) or 360 months (30 years). The longer the time horizon, the lower the monthly income derived from the assets. Conversely, a shorter time horizon results in higher monthly income but may be considered riskier. Lenders choose these timeframes based on their risk tolerance, the borrower's age, and the overall loan profile. Understanding how this variable works can help borrowers strategically position their assets to achieve the best possible outcome.

In addition to accessibility and time horizon, lenders also evaluate the stability and composition of the assets themselves. Not all retirement accounts are created equal. Accounts heavily invested in volatile assets may be viewed more conservatively than those with a balanced or conservative allocation. For example, a portfolio consisting primarily of high-risk stocks may be discounted more aggressively than one that includes bonds or diversified mutual funds. This does not mean that higher-risk portfolios cannot be used, but it does mean that the borrower may need to accept a lower qualifying income as a result. Documentation is another cornerstone of the evaluation process. Lenders require clear, consistent, and verifiable evidence of the assets being used for qualification. This typically includes recent account statements, proof of ownership, and sometimes a history of account activity. Any inconsistencies or unexplained changes in account balances can raise red flags and delay the approval process. Borrowers who take the time to organize and present their financial information clearly often experience a much smoother underwriting process.

Lenders also consider the concept of continuity. Even if a borrower has substantial assets, the lender must be confident that those assets will remain available over time. This means evaluating not only the current balance but also the borrower's withdrawal strategy, investment approach, and overall financial plan. If a borrower is withdrawing large amounts from their accounts or engaging in high-risk investment behavior, the lender may view the assets as less reliable, which could impact the final qualifying income.

Another important aspect of evaluation is the interaction between assets and liabilities. Lenders do not evaluate assets in isolation; they consider them in the context of the borrower's overall financial profile. This includes existing debts, credit obligations, and the proposed mortgage payment. The goal is to determine whether the borrower's assets can support all of these obligations over time. A borrower with significant assets but equally significant liabilities may still face challenges in qualifying, depending on how these factors balance out.

It is also worth noting that different lenders and loan programs may have different guidelines for evaluating retirement assets. Some lenders specialize in asset-based lending and may offer more flexible or favorable terms, while others may adhere more strictly to traditional underwriting standards. This variability underscores the importance of working with knowledgeable professionals who understand the nuances of asset-based qualification and can guide borrowers toward the most appropriate options.

As borrowers gain a deeper understanding of how lenders evaluate retirement accounts, they can begin to think more strategically about how to structure their financial profiles. This includes decisions about when to consolidate accounts, how to allocate investments, and whether to begin taking distributions. Each of these choices can have a direct impact on how the borrower is perceived by the lender and, ultimately, on the likelihood of approval.

At its core, the evaluation of retirement assets is about risk management. Lenders are not simply looking for wealth; they are looking for sustainable, accessible, and well-documented wealth that can reliably support mortgage payments over time. By understanding the criteria that lenders use to assess these factors, borrowers can position themselves more effectively and navigate the qualification process with greater confidence.

Real-Life Math Example: Lender Evaluation of Retirement Assets in Practice

Consider a borrower named Susan, who is 58 years old and planning to purchase a new primary residence. Susan has recently stepped away from full-time employment and does not have a traditional income source. However, she has accumulated significant retirement savings over the years. Her financial profile includes $900,000 in a traditional IRA, $300,000 in a Roth IRA, and $200,000 in a taxable brokerage account. In total, Susan has $1,400,000 in assets.

The lender begins by evaluating the accessibility of Susan's accounts. Since she is under 59½, the traditional IRA is subject to potential early withdrawal penalties, which increases the perceived risk. As a result, the lender applies a 40% discount to the traditional IRA, reducing its usable value to $540,000. The Roth IRA, while still subject to some restrictions, is treated more favorably due to its tax advantages, and a 15% discount is applied, resulting in $255,000. The brokerage account, being fully liquid, is used at

100% of its value, contributing $200,000. After these adjustments, Susan's total usable assets equal $995,000. The lender then determines the appropriate time horizon for asset depletion. Given Susan's age and the loan program guidelines, a 30-year (360-month) period is selected. Dividing $995,000 by 360 results in a monthly income of approximately $2,764.

Susan also receives a small pension of $1,200 per month, which is added to her asset-based income. This brings her total qualifying income to $3,964 per month. The lender then reviews her liabilities, which include a car payment of $350 and credit card obligations totaling $150 per month. Her total monthly debt is $500.

Next, the lender calculates Susan's debt-to-income ratio. With $500 in monthly debt and $3,964 in income, her ratio is approximately 12.6%, which is well within acceptable limits. Based on this analysis, Susan appears to be a strong candidate for mortgage approval.

However, the lender also considers alternative scenarios to assess risk. For example, if the market were to decline and Susan's portfolio lost 20% of its value, her adjusted assets would decrease to $796,000. Dividing this amount over 360 months would result in a monthly income of approximately $2,211. Adding her pension, her total income would be $3,411, still sufficient to support her current debt obligations. This stress test provides additional confidence to the lender that Susan's assets are robust enough to withstand market fluctuations while still supporting her mortgage payments. It also highlights the importance of conservative assumptions in the underwriting process.

Through this example, it becomes clear that lender evaluation is not just about calculating numbers—it is about understanding the full financial picture, applying appropriate adjustments, and ensuring that the borrower's assets can provide long-term stability. By aligning her financial profile with the lender's expectations, Susan is able to secure financing and move forward with her home purchase, even without traditional income.

Chapter 3

Structuring Retirement Assets for Maximum Mortgage Qualification

Once a borrower understands how lenders evaluate retirement accounts, the next step is learning how to strategically structure those assets to maximize qualifying income. This is where the process shifts from passive understanding to active optimization. Many borrowers assume that simply having a large amount of money in retirement accounts is enough to qualify, but in reality, how those assets are organized, allocated, and presented can significantly impact the outcome. Small structural decisions can mean the difference between approval and denial, or between qualifying for a modest loan versus a significantly larger one.

The first principle of structuring retirement assets is clarity. Lenders want to see clean, organized, and easily verifiable accounts. When assets are scattered across multiple institutions, accounts, and investment vehicles, it can create confusion and slow down the underwriting process. Consolidation, when done strategically, can simplify documentation and make it easier for lenders to evaluate the total asset picture. This does not mean that all assets must be combined into a single account, but rather that the borrower should present them in a way that clearly demonstrates ownership, accessibility, and stability.

The second principle is accessibility optimization. As discussed in the previous chapter, lenders place significant weight on how accessible retirement funds are. Borrowers who are close to or above retirement age often have an advantage because they can access their funds without penalties. However, even younger borrowers can improve their position by structuring their accounts in a way that increases perceived accessibility. For example, maintaining a portion of assets in brokerage accounts or other liquid investments can enhance the overall profile, as these funds are immediately available without restrictions. This balance between retirement and non-retirement assets can create a more favorable evaluation.

Another important strategy involves timing distributions. In some cases, borrowers may benefit from initiating structured withdrawals from their retirement accounts before applying for a mortgage. By establishing a consistent distribution history, they can create a verifiable income stream that lenders may treat similarly to traditional income. However, this approach must be used carefully. Unnecessary withdrawals can trigger taxes and reduce long-term wealth. The key is to align distribution strategies with both short-term qualification goals and long-term financial planning. Asset allocation also plays a critical role in how retirement accounts are perceived by lenders. A portfolio that is heavily concentrated in high-volatility investments may be subject to larger discounts during underwriting. On the other hand, a diversified portfolio that includes a mix of equities, bonds, and stable income-producing assets may be viewed as more reliable. While borrowers should not drastically alter their investment strategy solely for mortgage qualification, modest adjustments that improve stability and reduce perceived risk can be beneficial.

Another advanced concept in structuring is the segmentation of assets. Instead of viewing all assets as a single pool, borrowers can think of their portfolio in layers. One layer may be dedicated to long-term growth, another to income generation, and another to liquidity. By clearly defining these layers, borrowers can present a more strategic and intentional financial profile. Lenders are more likely to view such a profile favorably because it demonstrates planning, discipline, and a clear understanding of financial management.

The seasoning of assets is another critical factor. Lenders typically prefer assets that have been held in an account for a certain period of time, often 60 days or more. Recently transferred or deposited funds may require additional documentation to verify their source, which can complicate the process. Borrowers who plan ahead and ensure that their assets are properly seasoned before applying for a mortgage can avoid unnecessary delays and scrutiny.

In addition to seasoning, the titling of accounts can also impact qualification. Accounts held in the borrower's name are generally easier to use for qualification purposes than those held jointly or in the name of a business or trust. While it is still possible to use jointly held or trust-owned assets, doing so may require additional documentation and legal verification. Understanding these nuances allows borrowers to position their assets in the most favorable way possible.

Another often overlooked strategy is reducing liabilities before applying. While this chapter focuses on assets, it is important to remember that lenders evaluate the entire financial picture. By paying down or eliminating certain debts, borrowers can improve their debt-to-income ratio, which in turn increases their borrowing capacity. In some cases, using a small portion of assets to eliminate high-interest debt can have a disproportionately positive impact on overall qualification.

Borrowers should also consider the role of reserves. Many lenders require borrowers to have a certain number of months' worth of mortgage payments available as reserves after closing. Structuring assets in a way that clearly satisfies these reserve requirements can strengthen the application and provide additional confidence to the lender. This may involve setting aside a specific portion of assets in highly liquid accounts that are designated for this purpose.

Another key element of structuring is working with the right professionals. Not all lenders and loan officers have experience with asset-based mortgage qualification. Borrowers who work with professionals who understand these strategies can benefit from more accurate guidance, better loan options, and a smoother overall process. This includes not only mortgage professionals but also financial advisors who can help align investment strategies with borrowing goals.

As borrowers implement these structuring strategies, they begin to move from a reactive position to a proactive one. Instead of simply submitting their financial information and hoping for approval, they take control of how their profile is presented and evaluated. This level of control can lead to better outcomes, greater confidence, and a more efficient path to homeownership.

Ultimately, structuring retirement assets is about creating a narrative that aligns with lender expectations. It is about demonstrating that the borrower's wealth is not only substantial but also stable, accessible, and sustainable. By understanding and applying the principles outlined in this chapter, borrowers can unlock the full potential of their assets and position themselves for success in the mortgage qualification process.

Real-Life Math Example: Structuring Assets to Increase Qualifying Income

Consider a borrower named David, who is 60 years old and preparing to purchase a home. David has accumulated significant retirement savings but initially struggles to qualify for the loan amount he desires. His original asset profile includes $1,000,000 in a traditional IRA and $100,000 in a checking account. In total, he has $1,100,000 in assets.

The lender begins by evaluating David's accounts. Because the majority of his assets are in a traditional IRA, a 35% discount is applied to account for taxes and potential risks. This reduces the usable value of the IRA to $650,000. The checking account is fully liquid and used at 100%, contributing $100,000. David's total usable assets are therefore $750,000.

The lender then applies a 30-year (360-month) asset depletion calculation. Dividing $750,000 by 360 results in a monthly income of approximately $2,083. David has no additional income sources, and his monthly debts total $600. This results in a debt-to-income ratio that limits his borrowing capacity, preventing him from qualifying for the home he wants.

Recognizing this limitation, David works with a financial advisor to restructure his assets. He reallocates $200,000 from his traditional IRA into a brokerage account, accepting the tax implications as part of a broader strategy. His new asset profile includes $800,000 in a traditional IRA, $200,000 in a brokerage account, and $100,000 in checking.

The lender reevaluates his assets. The traditional IRA is still discounted by 35%, resulting in $520,000. The brokerage account is used at 100%, contributing $200,000, and the checking account adds another $100,000. David's total usable assets are now $820,000.

Dividing $820,000 by 360 months results in a monthly income of approximately $2,278. While this increase may seem modest, it improves his debt-to-income ratio enough to expand his borrowing capacity. Additionally, the presence of a larger liquid asset base improves the lender's perception of his financial stability.

David takes the strategy one step further by paying off a $300 monthly car payment using a portion of his checking account. This reduces his total monthly debt to $300. With a higher qualifying income and lower debt, his debt-to-income ratio improves significantly, allowing him to qualify for the desired loan amount. This example demonstrates how strategic structuring can have a meaningful impact on mortgage qualification. By reallocating assets, improving liquidity, and reducing liabilities, David transforms his financial profile and achieves his goal. It highlights the importance of not just having assets, but using them intelligently to align with lender expectations and maximize opportunities.

Chapter 4

Using Retirement Assets to Purchase or Refinance a Primary Residence

The transition from understanding and structuring retirement assets to actually using them in a real mortgage transaction is where theory becomes reality. For many borrowers, this is the most important stage of the entire process. It is one thing to know that retirement assets can be used for qualification, but it is another to successfully apply those assets toward purchasing or refinancing a primary residence. This chapter focuses on how retirement-based qualification is implemented in real-world scenarios, including how lenders assess risk, structure loan approvals, and determine the borrower's ability to sustain homeownership over time.

When a borrower applies for a mortgage using retirement assets, the lender's primary concern is sustainability. Unlike traditional income, which is assumed to continue as long as employment remains stable, retirement assets must be carefully evaluated to ensure they will last throughout the life of the loan. The lender is not just asking whether the borrower can make the first payment, but whether they can make every payment over the next 10, 20, or 30 years. This long-term perspective shapes every aspect of the underwriting process.

For primary residences, lenders tend to apply slightly more flexible guidelines compared to investment properties because the borrower is expected to live in the home. However, this flexibility does not eliminate risk considerations. In fact, lenders often take a deeper look at the borrower's overall financial stability when retirement assets are the primary source of qualification. This includes evaluating not only the total asset base but also how those assets are managed, accessed, and preserved.

One of the first decisions borrowers must make is whether to purchase a home or refinance an existing one. While both scenarios involve similar qualification methods, the goals and strategies can differ significantly. In a purchase transaction, the borrower is typically focused on maximizing buying power while maintaining financial security. In a refinance scenario, the borrower may be looking to reduce monthly payments, access equity, or restructure existing debt. Each objective requires a slightly different approach to asset utilization.

In a purchase scenario, retirement assets are used to establish qualifying income, which determines how much the borrower can afford. The lender calculates a monthly income figure using asset depletion or documented distributions, then compares it to the proposed housing payment and other debts. The key is ensuring that the borrower's debt-to-income ratio falls within acceptable limits. Because retirement-based income can sometimes be lower than traditional employment income, borrowers must be strategic in selecting a purchase price that aligns with their qualifying profile.

Down payment strategy also plays a critical role. Borrowers using retirement assets must decide how much of their funds to allocate toward the down payment versus how much to retain for qualification purposes. A larger down payment reduces the loan amount and monthly payment, which can improve approval chances. However, it also reduces the asset base used to calculate qualifying income. Finding the right balance is essential. In many cases, borrowers benefit from making a moderate down payment while preserving enough assets to support a strong income calculation.

In a refinance scenario, the focus often shifts to optimizing cash flow. Borrowers may use retirement assets to qualify for a lower interest rate, extend the loan term, or consolidate debt. In some cases, they may pursue a cash-out refinance to access equity for other investments or financial needs. The challenge in these situations is ensuring that the use of assets enhances overall financial stability rather than creating additional risk. Lenders will closely evaluate how the refinance impacts the borrower's long-term financial position. Another important consideration is reserves. For primary residence loans, lenders typically require borrowers to have a certain number of months' worth of mortgage payments available after closing. Retirement assets can often be used to satisfy this requirement, but the lender must be confident that these funds are accessible and sufficient. Strong reserves not only improve approval chances but may also lead to better loan terms, as they reduce the perceived risk of default.

Interest rates and loan terms are also influenced by how retirement assets are used in qualification. Borrowers with strong asset profiles and low debt-to-income ratios may qualify for more favorable rates, even without traditional income. Conversely, borrowers with marginal asset-based income may face slightly higher rates or stricter conditions. Understanding this relationship allows borrowers to make informed decisions about loan structure and timing.

Tax implications are another critical factor when using retirement assets. While asset depletion does not require actual withdrawals, any funds used for down payments, closing costs, or reserves may have tax consequences depending on the account type. Borrowers must consider how these withdrawals will affect their overall financial plan, including potential tax liabilities and future retirement income. Coordinating with a financial advisor can help ensure that mortgage decisions align with long-term financial goals.

Timing is also a key element in successfully using retirement assets for a mortgage. Market conditions, interest rates, and personal financial circumstances all play a role in determining the optimal time to buy or refinance. Additionally, the timing of asset transfers, distributions, and account adjustments can impact how the lender evaluates the borrower's profile. Planning ahead and allowing sufficient time for assets to be properly structured and seasoned can significantly improve the outcome.

As borrowers navigate this process, they begin to see that using retirement assets for a primary residence is not just about qualification—it is about strategy. It requires a holistic view of finances, including assets, liabilities, goals, and risk tolerance. By approaching the process with a clear plan and a deep understanding of lender expectations, borrowers can leverage their assets to achieve homeownership while maintaining financial security.

Ultimately, the use of retirement assets in purchasing or refinancing a primary residence represents a powerful opportunity. It allows borrowers to access real estate without being constrained by traditional income requirements, opening doors that might otherwise remain closed. However, this opportunity comes with responsibility. Borrowers must ensure that their decisions support long-term stability and align with their overall financial objectives. As you move forward, remember that your retirement assets are more than just savings for the future—they are tools that can be used strategically in the present. When applied correctly, they can provide access, flexibility, and control in the mortgage process, enabling you to achieve your housing goals on your own terms.

Real-Life Math Example: Purchasing a Primary Residence Using Retirement Assets

Consider a borrower named Linda, who is 64 years old and recently retired. Linda owns her current home free and clear but wants to purchase a new primary residence closer to her family. She plans to sell her existing home after securing the new one. Linda does not have employment income, but she has accumulated significant retirement savings, including $1,200,000 in a traditional IRA, $300,000 in a Roth IRA, and $200,000 in a brokerage account.

Linda is interested in purchasing a home priced at $600,000. She plans to make a 20% down payment of $120,000, leaving a loan amount of $480,000. Before moving forward, the lender must determine whether Linda can qualify for this loan using her retirement assets.

The lender begins by evaluating Linda's assets. The traditional IRA is discounted by 30% to account for taxes, resulting in a usable value of $840,000. The Roth IRA is discounted by 10%, resulting in $270,000. The brokerage account is used at 100%, contributing $200,000. This brings Linda's total usable assets to $1,310,000.

However, the lender must also account for the $120,000 down payment, which will be deducted from her available assets. After subtracting this amount, Linda's remaining usable assets equal $1,190,000. The lender then applies a 30-year (360-month) asset depletion calculation. Dividing $1,190,000 by 360 results in a monthly income of approximately $3,306.

Linda also receives Social Security income of $2,000 per month, bringing her total qualifying income to $5,306. The lender then calculates her proposed housing payment, including principal, interest, taxes, and insurance, which totals $2,800 per month. Linda has no other significant debts.

To determine her eligibility, the lender calculates her debt-to-income ratio. With a housing payment of $2,800 and total income of $5,306, her ratio is approximately 52.8%. While this is on the higher end, some lenders may still approve the loan due to her strong asset profile and lack of additional debt.

To improve her position, Linda considers increasing her down payment to $180,000, reducing the loan amount to $420,000.

This lowers her monthly housing payment to approximately $2,400. After adjusting for the larger down payment, her remaining usable assets equal $1,130,000. Dividing this amount by 360 results in a monthly income of approximately $3,139. Adding her Social Security income, her total qualifying income becomes $5,139.

With a lower housing payment of $2,400 and income of $5,139, her debt-to-income ratio improves to approximately 46.7%, making her a stronger candidate for approval. Additionally, the lower loan amount reduces the lender's risk, which may result in better loan terms.

This example illustrates how retirement assets can be used strategically to purchase a primary residence. By adjusting her down payment and understanding how her assets are evaluated, Linda is able to position herself for a successful mortgage approval. It also highlights the importance of balancing asset usage with long-term financial stability, ensuring that she retains sufficient resources for future needs while achieving her housing goals.

Chapter 5

Using Retirement Assets to Build an Investment Property Portfolio

As borrowers become more advanced in asset-based mortgage strategies, the natural progression is moving beyond a primary residence and into investment properties. This is where retirement assets can become not just a tool for qualification, but a catalyst for long-term wealth creation. While using assets to purchase a home provides stability and lifestyle benefits, using those same assets to acquire income-producing real estate introduces leverage, scalability, and the potential for compounding returns. However, qualifying for investment properties using retirement assets requires a deeper level of strategy, as lenders apply stricter guidelines and higher risk standards compared to primary residence loans.

The first major distinction borrowers must understand is that investment property loans are inherently riskier in the eyes of lenders. Unlike a primary residence, where the borrower has a personal incentive to maintain payments, investment properties are viewed as optional obligations. If financial challenges arise, borrowers are statistically more likely to default on investment properties before their primary home. As a result, lenders compensate for this increased risk by tightening underwriting criteria, requiring higher credit scores, larger down payments, stronger reserves, and more conservative income calculations.

When retirement assets are used to qualify for an investment property, lenders place even greater emphasis on sustainability and liquidity. It is no longer enough to demonstrate that assets exist; borrowers must show that those assets can support both the new property and any existing obligations over time. This includes accounting for vacancies, maintenance costs, and potential fluctuations in rental income. The lender's goal is to ensure that the borrower can withstand periods of reduced cash flow without jeopardizing the loan.

One of the most important concepts in investment property qualification is the interaction between asset-based income and rental income. In many cases, lenders will allow a portion of the expected rental income from the property to be included in the borrower's qualifying income. However, this income is typically discounted—often by 25%—to account for vacancies and expenses. When combined with asset depletion income, this creates a hybrid income model that can significantly enhance borrowing capacity if structured correctly.

Down payment requirements for investment properties are generally higher than for primary residences, often ranging from 20% to 30% or more. This requirement directly impacts how retirement assets are used. Borrowers must carefully decide how much to allocate toward the down payment versus how much to retain for qualification purposes. A larger down payment reduces the loan amount and monthly payment, which can improve debt-to-income ratios. However, it also reduces the asset base used to generate qualifying income. This trade-off must be evaluated strategically to achieve the optimal balance.

Reserves play an even more critical role in investment property loans. Lenders often require six to twelve months of mortgage payments as reserves for each property owned, including the new one. These reserves must typically be held in liquid or near-liquid accounts, which means that not all retirement assets may qualify. Borrowers who plan ahead and allocate a portion of their assets to meet these reserve requirements can significantly strengthen their application.

Another key factor is portfolio scalability. Borrowers who intend to acquire multiple investment properties must think beyond a single transaction. Each new property adds to the overall debt load and reserve requirements, which can impact future qualification. Structuring retirement assets in a way that supports multiple acquisitions requires careful planning, including maintaining sufficient liquidity, managing debt levels, and optimizing asset allocation. This forward-thinking approach allows borrowers to build a portfolio over time without hitting qualification limits prematurely.

Lenders also evaluate the borrower's experience with real estate investing. While not always required, a track record of successfully managing properties can improve the lender's confidence and potentially lead to more favorable terms. For borrowers new to investing, demonstrating a strong financial profile and a clear plan for managing the property can help offset the lack of experience.

Another advanced strategy involves leveraging equity from existing properties in combination with retirement assets. Borrowers who own real estate may be able to access equity through refinancing or home equity lines of credit, using those funds in conjunction with retirement assets to acquire additional properties. This layered approach can accelerate portfolio growth, but it also increases complexity and risk, requiring careful management and planning.

Tax considerations become even more important when retirement assets are used for investment purposes. Withdrawals from certain accounts may trigger taxes, which can reduce the effective value of the assets. Additionally, rental income introduces new tax implications, including depreciation, deductions, and potential capital gains. Borrowers must consider how these factors interact with their overall financial strategy and long-term goals.

Market conditions also play a significant role in investment property decisions. Interest rates, property values, rental demand, and economic trends all influence the viability of an investment. Borrowers using retirement assets must be particularly mindful of these factors, as their financial flexibility may be more limited compared to those with active income streams. Timing and location become critical components of a successful investment strategy.

As borrowers move into the realm of investment properties, they begin to see that asset-based mortgage qualification is not just a financing tool—it is a wealth-building system. By leveraging retirement assets strategically, they can acquire income-producing properties that generate cash flow, appreciate in value, and create long-term financial security. However, this system requires discipline, planning, and a deep understanding of both lending guidelines and investment principles.

Ultimately, the goal is not just to acquire properties, but to build a sustainable and scalable portfolio that aligns with the borrower's financial objectives. Retirement assets provide the foundation, but it is the strategic use of those assets that determines success. By mastering the concepts in this chapter, borrowers can transition from passive savers to active investors, using their wealth to create new opportunities and expand their financial horizons.

Real-Life Math Example: Using Retirement Assets to Acquire an Investment Property

Consider a borrower named Robert, who is 63 years old and interested in purchasing his first investment property. Robert has $1,500,000 in retirement assets, consisting of $1,000,000 in a traditional IRA, $300,000 in a Roth IRA, and $200,000 in a brokerage account. He also owns his primary residence outright and has no significant debt.

Robert identifies a rental property priced at $400,000. The lender requires a 25% down payment, which amounts to $100,000. This leaves a loan amount of $300,000. The estimated monthly mortgage payment, including taxes and insurance, is $2,200.

The lender begins by evaluating Robert's assets. The traditional IRA is discounted by 30%, resulting in a usable value of $700,000. The Roth IRA is discounted by 10%, resulting in $270,000. The brokerage account is used at 100%, contributing $200,000. This brings Robert's total usable assets to $1,170,000. After subtracting the $100,000 down payment, Robert's remaining usable assets equal $1,070,000. The lender applies a 30-year (360-month) asset depletion calculation, resulting in a monthly income of approximately $2,972.

Next, the lender considers the rental income from the property. The property is expected to generate $2,500 per month in rent. Applying a 25% vacancy and expense factor, the lender uses 75% of this amount, or $1,875, as qualifying rental income.

Robert's total qualifying income is therefore $2,972 (asset-based income) plus $1,875 (rental income), for a total of $4,847 per month. Since Robert has no other debts, the lender compares this income to the proposed housing payment of $2,200.

The resulting debt-to-income ratio is approximately 45.4%, which is within acceptable limits for many investment property loan programs. Additionally, the lender requires six months of reserves, which amounts to $13,200. Robert's remaining assets far exceed this requirement, further strengthening his application.

Now consider how Robert could scale this strategy. If he purchases a second property with similar numbers, his total rental income would double, but so would his debt obligations and reserve requirements. His asset base would decrease due to additional down payments, which could reduce his asset-based income. To maintain qualification, Robert would need to carefully manage these variables, ensuring that his income continues to exceed his obligations.

This example demonstrates how retirement assets can be used not only to qualify for an investment property but also to build a foundation for a larger portfolio. By combining asset-based income with rental income and maintaining strong reserves, Robert is able to enter the real estate market and begin generating additional income streams. It highlights the importance of strategic planning, balance, and long-term thinking in achieving success with asset-based mortgage lending.

Chapter 6

Securities-Based Mortgage Lending Strategies Using Retirement and Investment Accounts

As borrowers advance further into asset-based mortgage strategies, they begin to encounter one of the most powerful and sophisticated tools available: securities-based lending. Unlike traditional asset depletion models that convert retirement savings into qualifying income, securities-based strategies focus on leveraging the value of investment accounts—such as stocks, bonds, mutual funds, and managed portfolios—without necessarily liquidating them. This allows borrowers to maintain their investment positions while simultaneously accessing financing for real estate, creating a dual benefit of continued market participation and real estate acquisition.

Securities-based mortgage lending operates on a simple but powerful principle: your investments can serve as collateral. Instead of selling assets and triggering taxes or disrupting long-term growth, borrowers can use the value of their portfolios to support a loan. This approach is particularly attractive to high-net-worth individuals and experienced investors who understand the importance of keeping capital invested. Over time, the ability to remain in the market while acquiring appreciating real estate assets can significantly enhance overall wealth accumulation.

One of the most common forms of securities-based lending is a securities-backed line of credit, often referred to as an SBLOC. While this is not a mortgage itself, it can be used in conjunction with mortgage financing or as a bridge to acquire property. Lenders evaluate the borrower's investment portfolio and extend a line of credit based on a percentage of the portfolio's value, often ranging from 50% to 70%, depending on the asset composition. More stable portfolios with diversified holdings may qualify for higher leverage, while more volatile portfolios may receive lower advance rates.

In the context of mortgage lending, securities can also be used to strengthen a borrower's financial profile. For example, a borrower with a large brokerage account may not need to rely solely on asset depletion calculations. Instead, the lender may consider the account as a source of liquidity, reserves, or even supplemental income. This can result in more favorable loan terms, higher borrowing capacity, and increased flexibility in structuring the loan.

However, securities-based strategies come with unique risks that must be carefully managed. One of the most significant risks is market volatility. Because the value of the portfolio serves as the foundation for the loan, fluctuations in the market can impact the borrower's borrowing capacity and overall financial stability. In extreme cases, a significant decline in portfolio value could trigger a margin call or require the borrower to provide additional collateral. This risk underscores the importance of maintaining a diversified and well-managed portfolio.

Another key consideration is the type of assets held within the portfolio. Not all securities are treated equally by lenders. Blue-chip stocks, government bonds, and diversified mutual funds are generally viewed more favorably than speculative or highly concentrated investments. Lenders may apply different advance rates or discounts depending on the composition of the portfolio. Borrowers who understand these distinctions can structure their investments in a way that maximizes their borrowing potential while minimizing risk.

Tax efficiency is another major advantage of securities-based strategies. By avoiding the liquidation of assets, borrowers can defer capital gains taxes and maintain the compounding effect of their investments. This can be particularly beneficial for long-term investors who have built significant unrealized gains over time. However, borrowers must also consider the interest costs associated with securities-based loans and how those costs compare to potential investment returns.

Integration with retirement accounts adds another layer of complexity. While certain retirement accounts cannot be directly pledged as collateral, they can still play a role in the overall strategy. For example, a borrower may use a brokerage account as collateral while relying on retirement accounts for additional reserves or income qualification. This layered approach allows borrowers to optimize different types of assets for different purposes, creating a more efficient and flexible financial structure.

Another advanced strategy involves using securities-based lending to fund down payments or bridge financing. Instead of withdrawing funds from retirement accounts or selling investments, a borrower can use an SBLOC to access the necessary capital quickly. Once the property is acquired, the borrower can refinance into a traditional or asset-based mortgage, repaying the line of credit. This approach can be particularly useful in competitive real estate markets where speed and liquidity are critical.

Lenders also evaluate the relationship between the borrower's securities and their overall financial profile. A borrower with a large, well-managed portfolio and minimal debt is often viewed as a low-risk candidate, even without traditional income. This can lead to more favorable loan terms, including lower interest rates and higher loan-to-value ratios. Conversely, a borrower with a highly leveraged or volatile portfolio may face stricter conditions.

Risk management is central to any securities-based strategy. Borrowers must consider not only the potential benefits but also the potential downsides, including market downturns, interest rate changes, and liquidity constraints. Maintaining a buffer of unencumbered assets, diversifying investments, and avoiding excessive leverage are all critical components of a sustainable strategy.

As borrowers gain experience with securities-based lending, they begin to see it as part of a broader financial ecosystem. It is not a standalone solution but rather a complementary tool that can be integrated with other strategies, such as asset depletion, rental income, and traditional financing. By combining these approaches, borrowers can create a highly customized financing plan that aligns with their goals and risk tolerance.

Ultimately, securities-based mortgage strategies offer a powerful way to unlock the value of investment portfolios without sacrificing long-term growth. They provide flexibility, efficiency, and the potential for enhanced returns, but they also require a high level of discipline and understanding. Borrowers who master these strategies can position themselves at the forefront of modern lending, using their assets not just as a safety net, but as a dynamic tool for building wealth.

Real-Life Math Example: Leveraging Securities to Acquire Real Estate Without Liquidation

Consider a borrower named Karen, who is 55 years old and has built a substantial investment portfolio over the years. Her financial profile includes $2,000,000 in a diversified brokerage account, consisting of stocks, bonds, and mutual funds. She also has $800,000 in retirement accounts, but she prefers not to withdraw from them due to tax considerations and long-term growth objectives.

Karen wants to purchase a property priced at $700,000. Instead of selling her investments to fund the purchase, she decides to use a securities-based line of credit. The lender evaluates her brokerage account and offers a 60% advance rate, allowing her to access up to $1,200,000 in credit.

Karen draws $200,000 from the line of credit to use as a down payment, leaving her with a remaining credit capacity of

$1,000,000. She then applies for a mortgage for the remaining $500,000. The lender evaluates her financial profile, including her securities account, and determines that she qualifies based on her asset strength and liquidity.

The mortgage payment on the $500,000 loan is approximately $3,000 per month. In addition, Karen must pay interest on the $200,000 drawn from the line of credit. Assuming an interest rate of 6%, her monthly interest payment is approximately $1,000. Her total monthly obligation is therefore $4,000.

Karen's investment portfolio continues to generate returns. Assuming an average annual return of 7%, her $2,000,000 portfolio produces approximately $140,000 per year, or about $11,667 per month in growth. Even after accounting for market fluctuations, this level of return provides a strong buffer against her borrowing costs.

Now consider a scenario where the market declines by 15%, reducing her portfolio value to $1,700,000. The lender may reassess her borrowing capacity, but since she has only used a small portion of her available credit, she remains within acceptable limits. Her diversified portfolio and conservative use of leverage protect her from significant risk.

Over time, Karen has the option to refinance her mortgage, pay down the line of credit, or continue leveraging her portfolio for additional investments. By avoiding liquidation, she preserves her investment growth while acquiring real estate, effectively using her assets to work in multiple ways simultaneously.

This example illustrates the power of securities-based mortgage strategies. By leveraging her investment portfolio, Karen is able to acquire property without disrupting her long-term financial plan. It highlights the importance of balance, diversification, and strategic thinking in maximizing the benefits of asset-based lending while managing risk effectively.

Chapter 7

Foreign National Asset-Based Mortgage Strategies Using Global Retirement and Investment Assets

As the global economy becomes increasingly interconnected, real estate ownership in the United States has expanded far beyond domestic borrowers. International buyers—often referred to as foreign nationals—are actively purchasing residential and investment properties across the country, drawn by market stability, legal protections, and long-term appreciation potential. However, traditional mortgage qualification methods present significant barriers for these borrowers, primarily because they often lack U.S.-based income, credit history, or tax documentation. This is where asset-based mortgage strategies become not just useful, but essential.

Foreign national asset-based mortgage lending focuses on evaluating global wealth rather than local income. Instead of requiring U.S. tax returns or employment verification, lenders assess the borrower's financial strength based on assets held domestically or internationally. These assets may include foreign retirement accounts, investment portfolios, bank deposits, and business holdings. The challenge lies in translating these assets into a format that aligns with U.S. lending standards while managing the additional risks associated with cross-border transactions.

One of the first hurdles foreign national borrowers face is documentation. U.S. lenders require clear, verifiable evidence of asset ownership, which can be complicated when assets are held in foreign institutions. Documentation may need to be translated into English, converted into U.S. dollar equivalents, and verified through internationally recognized financial institutions. In some cases, lenders may require third-party validation or additional due diligence to confirm the legitimacy and stability of the assets.

Currency conversion is another critical factor. Assets held in foreign currencies must be converted into U.S. dollars for qualification purposes. However, lenders often apply conservative exchange rates or additional discounts to account for currency volatility. This ensures that the borrower's financial profile remains stable even if exchange rates fluctuate. Borrowers who understand this process can better anticipate how their assets will be evaluated and avoid surprises during underwriting. Accessibility remains a central concern, just as it does with domestic retirement assets. Lenders must determine whether the borrower can access their funds if needed, especially in the event of financial stress. Some foreign retirement accounts may have restrictions similar to U.S. accounts, including penalties for early withdrawal or limitations on international transfers. Lenders evaluate these factors carefully, often applying higher discounts to accounts that are less liquid or more difficult to access.

In addition to asset evaluation, lenders also consider geopolitical and regulatory risks. Assets held in countries with stable financial systems and strong legal protections are generally viewed more favorably than those in regions with higher economic or political uncertainty. This does not mean that assets from less stable regions cannot be used, but it may result in more conservative underwriting or additional documentation requirements.

Foreign national borrowers typically face higher down payment requirements, often ranging from 25% to 40% of the property value. This requirement serves as a risk mitigation tool for lenders, ensuring that the borrower has a significant financial stake in the property. While this may seem like a disadvantage, it also allows borrowers to leverage their assets more effectively, reducing the loan amount and improving overall qualification metrics. Another important aspect of foreign national lending is the absence of traditional credit history. Without a U.S. credit score, lenders must rely more heavily on asset strength and financial reserves to assess risk. In some cases, borrowers may provide international credit reports or banking references, but these are often supplementary rather than primary factors. A strong asset base can compensate for the lack of domestic credit, making asset-based strategies particularly valuable in this context.

Structuring becomes even more critical for foreign national borrowers. Assets must be organized in a way that demonstrates stability, accessibility, and compliance with U.S. lending standards. This may involve transferring funds to U.S.-based accounts, consolidating investments, or working with international financial institutions that have a presence in the United States. Proper structuring not only simplifies the underwriting process but also strengthens the borrower's overall profile.

Another advanced strategy involves using a combination of domestic and international assets. For example, a borrower may transfer a portion of their funds to a U.S. brokerage account while retaining the majority of their wealth overseas. This hybrid approach can improve liquidity and reduce perceived risk, while still leveraging the full asset base for qualification purposes. Tax considerations are also important for foreign national borrowers. While this book does not focus on tax advice, it is essential to understand that owning property in the United States may have tax implications, including withholding requirements, capital gains taxes, and reporting obligations. Borrowers should work with qualified professionals to ensure compliance and optimize their financial strategy.

Lenders also evaluate the intended use of the property. Primary residences, second homes, and investment properties each carry different risk profiles and qualification requirements. Foreign national borrowers often focus on investment properties or second homes, which may require additional reserves and stricter underwriting. Understanding these distinctions allows borrowers to align their strategy with lender expectations.

As global wealth continues to grow and diversify, foreign national asset-based mortgage strategies are becoming increasingly sophisticated. Lenders are developing specialized programs to accommodate international borrowers, recognizing the value of this market segment. These programs often include flexible documentation requirements, customized underwriting guidelines, and tailored loan structures designed to meet the unique needs of foreign nationals.

For borrowers, this represents a significant opportunity. By leveraging global assets, they can access one of the most stable and desirable real estate markets in the world. However, success requires careful planning, attention to detail, and a thorough understanding of both domestic and international financial systems.

Ultimately, foreign national asset-based mortgage lending is about bridging the gap between global wealth and local opportunity. It allows borrowers to translate their financial strength into real estate ownership, regardless of where their assets are held or how their income is structured. By mastering the concepts in this chapter, borrowers can navigate the complexities of cross-border lending and unlock new possibilities for growth and investment.

Real-Life Math Example: Using Global Assets to Qualify for a U.S. Investment Property

Consider a borrower named Carlos, who resides in Spain and is interested in purchasing an investment property in the United States. Carlos has no U.S. income or credit history, but he has built substantial wealth through business ownership and investments. His financial profile includes €900,000 in a European retirement account, €400,000 in a brokerage account, and €200,000 in cash savings. At the current exchange rate, these assets are equivalent to approximately

$1,500,000. The lender begins by evaluating Carlos's assets and converting them into U.S. dollars. To account for currency fluctuations, the lender applies a conservative adjustment, reducing the total value to $1,400,000. Next, the lender applies discounts based on accessibility and risk. The retirement account is discounted by 35%, resulting in $585,000. The brokerage account is discounted by 10%, resulting in $360,000. The cash savings are used at 100%, contributing $200,000. Carlos's total usable assets are therefore $1,145,000.

Carlos plans to purchase a property priced at $500,000. The lender requires a 30% down payment, which amounts to $150,000. After subtracting this amount from his usable assets, Carlos has $995,000 remaining for qualification purposes.

The lender applies a 30-year (360-month) asset depletion calculation. Dividing $995,000 by 360 results in a monthly income of approximately $2,764. Since Carlos has no other qualifying income, this figure becomes the basis for his debt-to-income evaluation.

The estimated monthly payment for the property, including taxes and insurance, is $2,200. With a qualifying income of $2,764, Carlos's debt-to-income ratio is approximately 79.6%, which is higher than typical guidelines. However, the lender also considers the expected rental income from the property, which is projected at $2,400 per month. Applying a 25% vacancy factor, the lender uses $1,800 as qualifying rental income.

Adding the rental income to the asset-based income results in a total qualifying income of $4,564 per month. With a monthly obligation of $2,200, Carlos's debt-to-income ratio improves to approximately 48.2%, making him a viable candidate for approval.

The lender also requires six months of reserves, totaling $13,200. Carlos's remaining assets far exceed this requirement, providing additional confidence in his ability to sustain the loan.

This example demonstrates how global assets can be effectively used to qualify for a U.S. mortgage, even in the absence of traditional income or credit history. By understanding how currency conversion, asset discounts, and rental income interact, Carlos is able to structure his financial profile in a way that meets lender requirements and achieves his investment goals.

Chapter 8

Jumbo Asset-Based Mortgage Loans for Luxury Real Estate

As borrowers progress into higher levels of asset-based mortgage strategies, they often encounter the world of jumbo lending—where loan amounts exceed conventional conforming limits and underwriting becomes more nuanced, more flexible, and more demanding at the same time. Jumbo asset-based mortgage loans represent a powerful opportunity for high-net-worth individuals to finance luxury real estate using their accumulated wealth rather than relying on traditional income. However, these loans require a deeper level of financial sophistication, as lenders are evaluating not just the borrower's ability to pay, but the sustainability, preservation, and strategic use of substantial assets over time.

Jumbo loans differ from standard mortgages in several key ways. First, they are not backed by government-sponsored entities, which means lenders assume more risk and therefore apply stricter internal guidelines. At the same time, because jumbo borrowers typically have strong financial profiles, lenders are often willing to offer more customized solutions. This creates a unique environment where flexibility and scrutiny coexist. Borrowers who understand how to navigate this environment can unlock significant advantages, including higher loan amounts, tailored loan structures, and access to premium properties.

When retirement assets are used to qualify for a jumbo mortgage, the scale of evaluation increases dramatically. Instead of assessing hundreds of thousands of dollars in assets, lenders may be reviewing portfolios in the millions. This requires a more detailed analysis of asset composition, diversification, and long-term sustainability. Lenders are particularly focused on ensuring that the borrower's wealth is not only sufficient to support the loan, but also resilient enough to withstand market fluctuations and economic uncertainty.

One of the defining characteristics of jumbo asset-based lending is the emphasis on asset quality. Lenders look closely at how assets are invested, not just how much exists. A well-diversified portfolio that includes equities, fixed income, and alternative investments may be viewed more favorably than a concentrated portfolio with higher volatility. This is because diversification reduces risk and increases the likelihood that the borrower's assets will maintain their value over time. Borrowers who proactively manage their portfolios with this in mind can improve their overall qualification profile. Liquidity becomes even more critical at the jumbo level. Lenders want to see that a borrower has access to sufficient liquid or near-liquid assets to cover not only the mortgage payments but also lifestyle expenses, property maintenance, and unforeseen financial needs. In many cases, lenders require significant reserves—sometimes 12 months or more of total housing payments. These reserves provide a safety net that reassures the lender of the borrower's ability to weather financial disruptions without defaulting.

Down payment requirements for jumbo loans are typically higher than for conforming loans, often ranging from 20% to 40% depending on the loan amount and borrower profile. This requirement serves multiple purposes. It reduces the lender's exposure, aligns the borrower's interests with the property, and ensures that the borrower retains a substantial asset base after closing. As with other asset-based strategies, borrowers must carefully balance the amount used for the down payment with the amount retained for qualification and reserves.

Another important aspect of jumbo lending is the customization of loan terms. Because these loans are not standardized, lenders may offer a variety of options, including adjustable-rate mortgages, interest-only periods, and flexible amortization schedules. These options can be particularly advantageous for borrowers who prefer to preserve liquidity or manage cash flow strategically. However, they also require a clear understanding of how different structures impact long-term financial outcomes.

Credit profile still plays a role in jumbo lending, even in asset-based scenarios. While strong assets can compensate for certain weaknesses, lenders generally expect higher credit scores and a history of responsible financial behavior. This is especially true for larger loan amounts, where the stakes are higher. Borrowers who maintain excellent credit can often secure better terms and more favorable interest rates.

Property type and location also influence jumbo loan approval. Luxury properties, unique homes, or properties in less conventional markets may require additional scrutiny. Lenders evaluate not only the borrower but also the asset being financed, ensuring that it retains value and can be resold if necessary. This dual evaluation adds another layer of complexity to the process.

Tax efficiency remains a key consideration when using retirement assets for jumbo loans. Large withdrawals to fund down payments or reserves can trigger significant tax liabilities, which may impact the borrower's overall financial position. Borrowers must carefully plan how funds are accessed, often coordinating with financial advisors to minimize tax impact while maintaining sufficient liquidity.

Another advanced strategy involves layering different types of assets to strengthen the overall profile. For example, a borrower may use a combination of retirement accounts, brokerage accounts, and real estate equity to support a jumbo loan. This diversified approach can enhance stability and reduce reliance on any single asset class, making the borrower more attractive to lenders.

Timing is particularly important in jumbo transactions. Market conditions, interest rates, and portfolio performance can all influence the optimal moment to secure financing. Borrowers who monitor these factors and act strategically can take advantage of favorable conditions, while those who rush into a transaction may face less optimal terms.

As borrowers move into the jumbo space, they begin to see that asset-based mortgage lending is not just about qualifying—it is about optimizing. It is about using wealth strategically to access opportunities, manage risk, and achieve long-term financial goals. Jumbo loans provide a platform for this optimization, allowing borrowers to leverage their assets in ways that align with their lifestyle and investment objectives.

Ultimately, jumbo asset-based mortgage loans represent the intersection of wealth management and real estate finance.

They require a high level of understanding, careful planning, and strategic execution. For those who master these elements, the rewards can be substantial, providing access to premium properties and the ability to maintain and grow wealth simultaneously.

Real-Life Math Example: Financing a Luxury Property Using Retirement and Investment Assets

Consider a borrower named James, who is 59 years old and has accumulated significant wealth over his career. His financial profile includes $3,000,000 in a traditional IRA, $1,000,000 in a Roth IRA, and $1,500,000 in a brokerage account. In total, James has $5,500,000 in assets.

James is interested in purchasing a luxury home priced at $2,000,000. The lender requires a 30% down payment, which amounts to $600,000. This leaves a loan amount of $1,400,000. The estimated monthly mortgage payment, including taxes and insurance, is $9,500.

The lender begins by evaluating James's assets. The traditional IRA is discounted by 30%, resulting in a usable value of $2,100,000. The Roth IRA is discounted by 10%, resulting in $900,000. The brokerage account is used at 100%, contributing $1,500,000. This brings James's total usable assets to $4,500,000.

After subtracting the $600,000 down payment, James's remaining usable assets equal $3,900,000. The lender applies a 30-year (360-month) asset depletion calculation. Dividing $3,900,000 by 360 results in a monthly income of approximately $10,833.

James also has no significant debt, which simplifies the analysis. With a monthly obligation of $9,500 and qualifying income of $10,833, his debt-to-income ratio is approximately 87.7%, which is higher than typical guidelines. However, the lender considers additional factors, including James's substantial reserves and overall financial strength.

To improve his profile, James decides to increase his down payment to $800,000, reducing the loan amount to $1,200,000 and the monthly payment to approximately $8,200. After adjusting for the larger down payment, his remaining usable assets equal $3,700,000. Dividing this amount by 360 results in a monthly income of approximately $10,278.

With a lower monthly payment of $8,200 and income of $10,278, his debt-to-income ratio improves to approximately 79.8%. While still high, his strong asset base, excellent credit, and significant reserves may allow the lender to approve the loan under a more flexible jumbo program.

Additionally, James's remaining assets provide more than 24 months of reserves, far exceeding typical requirements. This level of financial strength reassures the lender that he can sustain the loan even under adverse conditions.

This example illustrates the complexity and flexibility of jumbo asset-based mortgage lending. By adjusting his down payment and leveraging his diverse asset base, James is able to structure a loan that aligns with his goals while maintaining financial stability. It highlights the importance of strategic planning, asset management, and understanding lender expectations in achieving success at the highest levels of real estate financing.

Chapter 9

Asset-Based Mortgage Refinancing and Equity Access Strategies

As borrowers build equity in their properties and accumulate wealth through retirement and investment accounts, a new layer of opportunity emerges—refinancing and equity access. While purchasing a property using asset-based qualification is a powerful strategy, the ability to revisit that property later, unlock its value, and redeploy capital is where long-term financial leverage truly begins to accelerate. Refinancing is not just about lowering an interest rate; it is about restructuring debt, improving cash flow, accessing liquidity, and repositioning your overall financial strategy using both real estate equity and retirement assets.

In traditional lending, refinancing is often driven by income stability and improved credit profiles. However, in the asset-based world, the focus shifts toward total financial strength and strategic timing. Borrowers who may not have traditional income—or who prefer not to document it—can still refinance successfully by leveraging their retirement assets, investment portfolios, and accumulated property equity. This creates a unique advantage, allowing borrowers to make moves based on opportunity rather than being constrained by employment or tax documentation.

One of the most common reasons borrowers pursue refinancing is to reduce their monthly payment. This can be achieved by securing a lower interest rate, extending the loan term, or both. For asset-based borrowers, this is particularly valuable because it reduces the pressure on asset-derived income. By lowering the monthly obligation, borrowers can preserve more of their portfolio, extend the longevity of their assets, and improve overall financial stability. Even a modest reduction in monthly payments can have a significant long-term impact when viewed over the life of a loan.

Another powerful use of refinancing is cash-out equity access. Over time, as property values increase and loan balances decrease, borrowers build equity that can be converted into usable capital. A cash-out refinance allows borrowers to extract a portion of this equity while maintaining ownership of the property. When combined with asset-based qualification, this strategy becomes even more potent. Borrowers can access large amounts of capital without selling assets or triggering taxable events, then use that capital for investments, business opportunities, or additional real estate acquisitions.

However, accessing equity must be approached with discipline. While it may be tempting to maximize cash-out proceeds, doing so increases the loan balance and monthly payment, which can strain the borrower's financial profile. Lenders will evaluate whether the borrower's assets can support the new loan structure, including the increased obligations. The goal is to find a balance where equity is accessed efficiently without compromising long-term sustainability.

Rate-and-term refinancing is another important strategy. Unlike cash-out refinancing, this approach focuses on improving the terms of the existing loan without extracting additional funds. Borrowers may use this strategy to switch from an adjustable-rate mortgage to a fixed-rate loan, shorten the loan term, or eliminate mortgage insurance. For asset-based borrowers, this can be an effective way to stabilize long-term costs while maintaining flexibility in how assets are used.

Timing plays a critical role in refinancing decisions. Interest rate environments, property value trends, and portfolio performance all influence the optimal moment to refinance. Borrowers who monitor these factors and act strategically can capture significant financial benefits. For example, refinancing during a period of low interest rates can lock in long-term savings, while refinancing after a property has appreciated can increase available equity. Another key consideration is how refinancing interacts with retirement asset strategies. While asset depletion may be used for qualification, borrowers must ensure that their remaining assets are sufficient to support the new loan structure. This includes maintaining adequate reserves, preserving investment growth, and avoiding unnecessary withdrawals. In some cases, borrowers may choose to restructure their portfolios prior to refinancing to improve liquidity and reduce perceived risk.

Lenders also evaluate the purpose of the refinance. Using equity to acquire additional income-producing assets may be viewed more favorably than using it for discretionary spending. This is because income-generating investments can enhance the borrower's overall financial profile, while non-productive uses of funds may increase risk. Borrowers who clearly articulate their strategy and demonstrate how the refinance supports their long-term goals can strengthen their application.

Another advanced strategy involves combining refinancing with portfolio rebalancing. For example, a borrower may refinance a property to access equity, then use a portion of those funds to diversify their investment portfolio. This can reduce overall risk and create a more balanced financial structure. Alternatively, borrowers may use equity to pay down high-interest debt, improving cash flow and strengthening their debt-to-income ratio. Home equity lines of credit (HELOCs) and second mortgages also play a role in equity access strategies. While not always classified as traditional refinancing, these tools allow borrowers to tap into equity without replacing the existing mortgage. For asset-based borrowers, this can provide additional flexibility, especially when combined with strong asset reserves. However, these products often come with variable interest rates and require careful management.

As borrowers become more experienced, they begin to view refinancing not as a one-time event, but as an ongoing strategy. Each refinance decision becomes part of a larger financial plan, aligned with market conditions, investment opportunities, and personal goals. This mindset transforms refinancing from a reactive process into a proactive tool for wealth management.

Risk management remains a central theme throughout all refinancing strategies. Borrowers must consider how changes in interest rates, property values, and market conditions could impact their financial position. Maintaining a margin of safety—through reserves, diversification, and conservative leverage—is essential to ensuring long-term success.

Ultimately, asset-based mortgage refinancing and equity access strategies provide a powerful way to unlock the value of both real estate and financial assets. They allow borrowers to move capital efficiently, adapt to changing conditions, and pursue new opportunities without being constrained by traditional income requirements. When used thoughtfully, these strategies can accelerate wealth creation, enhance financial flexibility, and provide a level of control that is rarely achievable through conventional lending alone.

Real-Life Math Example: Cash-Out Refinancing Using Retirement Asset Qualification

Consider a borrower named Daniel, who is 61 years old and owns a home currently valued at $800,000. He purchased the home several years ago and now has a remaining loan balance of $300,000. This means he has $500,000 in equity. Daniel does not have traditional employment income, but he has substantial retirement savings, including $900,000 in a traditional IRA, $400,000 in a Roth IRA, and $200,000 in a brokerage account.

Daniel wants to access $200,000 of his home equity to invest in additional real estate opportunities. He applies for a cash-out refinance, which will increase his loan balance from $300,000 to $500,000. The new loan has an estimated monthly payment of $3,200.

The lender begins by evaluating Daniel's assets. The traditional IRA is discounted by 30%, resulting in a usable value of $630,000. The Roth IRA is discounted by 10%, resulting in $360,000. The brokerage account is used at 100%, contributing $200,000. This brings Daniel's total usable assets to $1,190,000.

The lender then applies a 30-year (360-month) asset depletion calculation. Dividing $1,190,000 by 360 results in a monthly income of approximately $3,306. Daniel also receives $1,500 per month in Social Security income, bringing his total qualifying income to $4,806.

Next, the lender evaluates the new mortgage payment of $3,200. Daniel has no other significant debts. His debt-to-income ratio is calculated by dividing $3,200 by $4,806, resulting in approximately 66.6%. While this is higher than typical guidelines, the lender considers Daniel's strong asset base and substantial remaining equity.

After the refinance, Daniel still has $300,000 in equity in the home, as well as over $1 million in adjusted assets. Additionally, he plans to use the $200,000 cash-out proceeds to purchase a rental property that is expected to generate $2,000 per month in income. Applying a 25% vacancy factor, the lender considers $1,500 of this as future qualifying income.

When this projected rental income is included, Daniel's total income increases to $6,306 per month. With a mortgage payment of $3,200, his adjusted debt-to-income ratio improves to approximately 50.7%, making the loan more viable. This example illustrates how refinancing and equity access can be used strategically in combination with retirement assets. By leveraging both his home equity and financial portfolio, Daniel is able to access capital, invest in additional income-producing assets, and strengthen his overall financial position. It highlights the importance of planning, balance, and understanding how different components of wealth interact within the asset-based lending framework.

Chapter 10

Advanced Asset-Based Mortgage Structuring and Strategic Positioning

As borrowers reach the highest level of asset-based mortgage mastery, the focus shifts from simply qualifying for loans to engineering approvals with precision. At this stage, the borrower is no longer reacting to lender requirements but proactively structuring their financial profile to achieve specific outcomes. Advanced asset-based mortgage structuring is about aligning assets, liabilities, timing, and strategy in a way that maximizes leverage, minimizes risk, and creates long-term financial control. This is where the true power of asset-based lending is unlocked.

The foundation of advanced structuring begins with understanding that lenders do not just evaluate numbers—they evaluate patterns, stability, and intent. A borrower with substantial assets may still be declined if those assets appear volatile, inaccessible, or poorly organized. Conversely, a borrower with a slightly smaller asset base may be approved if their financial profile demonstrates clarity, consistency, and sustainability. This means that presentation and positioning are just as important as the raw numbers themselves. One of the most powerful concepts in advanced structuring is layering income sources. Instead of relying on a single method of qualification, borrowers can combine asset depletion, retirement distributions, rental income, and even part-time or passive income streams. This layered approach creates a stronger and more flexible income profile, allowing borrowers to meet lender guidelines more easily. It also reduces reliance on any one source, improving overall stability and resilience.

Another critical strategy is optimizing the timing of financial moves. The sequence in which assets are transferred, debts are paid off, or distributions are initiated can significantly impact how a lender evaluates the borrower. For example, initiating consistent retirement distributions several months before applying for a mortgage can create a documented income stream that strengthens the application. Similarly, paying off certain debts prior to applying can improve debt-to-income ratios and increase borrowing capacity.

Advanced borrowers also understand the importance of asset positioning across different account types. Retirement accounts, brokerage accounts, cash reserves, and real estate equity each serve different roles in the qualification process. By allocating assets strategically across these categories, borrowers can maximize both qualifying income and liquidity. For example, maintaining a portion of assets in highly liquid accounts can satisfy reserve requirements, while larger retirement accounts can be used for asset depletion calculations.

Another key concept is minimizing friction in underwriting. Lenders prefer straightforward, well-documented financial profiles. Complex or unclear asset structures can create delays, additional documentation requests, or even denials. Advanced structuring involves simplifying where possible—consolidating accounts, ensuring proper titling, and clearly documenting the source and history of funds. This reduces uncertainty and allows the underwriter to focus on the strengths of the file.

Leverage optimization is also central to advanced strategies. Borrowers must decide how much debt to take on relative to their asset base. While higher leverage can increase returns, it also increases risk and may limit future borrowing capacity. Advanced borrowers carefully calibrate their leverage, ensuring that they maintain sufficient reserves and flexibility for future opportunities. This often involves running multiple scenarios to understand how different loan structures impact long-term outcomes.

Another sophisticated approach involves using assets to strategically eliminate liabilities. For example, paying off high-interest debt before applying for a mortgage can significantly improve debt-to-income ratios, making it easier to qualify for larger loans. In some cases, borrowers may use a small portion of their assets to eliminate multiple liabilities, creating a disproportionately positive impact on their overall financial profile.

Portfolio sequencing is another advanced concept. Borrowers who plan to acquire multiple properties or refinance over time must think about the order in which these transactions occur. Each transaction affects the borrower's financial profile, including asset levels, debt obligations, and reserve requirements. By sequencing transactions strategically, borrowers can maximize their borrowing capacity across multiple deals rather than limiting themselves with a single poorly timed decision.

Risk mitigation remains a cornerstone of all advanced strategies. Even as borrowers optimize their financial profiles, they must ensure that they are not overextending themselves. This includes maintaining adequate reserves, diversifying assets, and avoiding excessive reliance on volatile investments. A well-structured financial profile should be able to withstand market fluctuations, interest rate changes, and unexpected expenses without compromising stability.

Another important element is lender selection. Not all lenders are equally equipped to handle complex asset-based scenarios. Advanced borrowers often work with specialized lenders who understand these strategies and offer flexible underwriting guidelines. Choosing the right lender can significantly impact the outcome, including approval likelihood, loan terms, and overall experience.

Communication also plays a critical role. Borrowers who can clearly articulate their financial strategy and demonstrate a deep understanding of their own profile are more likely to gain the confidence of lenders and underwriters. This includes explaining how assets are structured, how income is generated, and how the loan fits into the broader financial plan. Clear communication reduces uncertainty and builds trust, which can be a deciding factor in complex cases.

As borrowers master these advanced techniques, they begin to operate at a different level. They are no longer constrained by traditional lending limitations but instead use their assets as a dynamic tool for creating opportunities. They can move capital efficiently, adapt to changing conditions, and structure deals that align with their long-term vision.

Ultimately, advanced asset-based mortgage structuring is about control. It is about taking ownership of the process, understanding every variable, and using that knowledge to achieve optimal outcomes. Whether the goal is to acquire multiple properties, refinance strategically, or preserve wealth while accessing liquidity, the principles in this chapter provide a roadmap for success.

Real-Life Math Example: Engineering a Mortgage Approval Through Advanced Structuring

Consider a borrower named Olivia, who is 57 years old and has a complex but strong financial profile. She has $1,800,000 in a traditional IRA, $600,000 in a Roth IRA, $400,000 in a brokerage account, and $200,000 in cash. She also owns a rental property generating $2,500 per month in income. Olivia wants to purchase a new property priced at $900,000.

Initially, Olivia struggles to qualify because her asset-based income alone is not sufficient to support the desired loan amount. The lender evaluates her assets and applies discounts: 30% to the traditional IRA, resulting in $1,260,000; 10% to the Roth IRA, resulting in $540,000; and 100% to the brokerage and cash accounts, contributing $600,000. Her total usable assets are $2,400,000.

Dividing this amount by 360 months results in a monthly income of approximately $6,667. Adding her rental income (adjusted to $1,875 after a 25% vacancy factor), her total qualifying income is $8,542. However, the projected mortgage payment for the new property is $5,500, and she has additional obligations totaling $1,000 per month, resulting in a debt-to-income ratio that is slightly above acceptable limits.

To improve her position, Olivia implements several advanced strategies. First, she pays off $500 in monthly debt using a portion of her cash reserves. This reduces her total monthly obligations. Next, she begins taking structured distributions from her Roth IRA, creating an additional documented income stream of $1,500 per month. She also reallocates $200,000 from her traditional IRA into her brokerage account, improving liquidity and reducing the overall discount applied to her assets.

After restructuring, the lender reevaluates her profile. Her adjusted assets now include a slightly lower traditional IRA balance but a higher proportion of liquid assets. Her asset-based income increases modestly due to improved weighting, and her total qualifying income rises to approximately $10,000 per month when combined with rental and distribution income.

With reduced debt and increased income, her debt-to-income ratio improves significantly, bringing her within acceptable guidelines. Additionally, her enhanced liquidity and reserves strengthen the overall application, giving the lender greater confidence in her ability to sustain the loan.

As a result, Olivia is approved for the mortgage and successfully acquires the property. This example demonstrates how advanced structuring can transform a marginal application into a strong one. By layering income sources, optimizing asset allocation, and strategically managing liabilities, Olivia is able to engineer an approval that aligns with her goals while maintaining financial stability.

This level of strategic thinking represents the pinnacle of asset-based mortgage mastery. It is not just about qualifying—it is about designing outcomes, controlling variables, and using financial knowledge to create opportunities that would otherwise remain out of reach.

Chapter 11

Long-Term Wealth Preservation and Risk Management with Asset-Based Mortgage Strategies

As borrowers master asset-based mortgage qualification and begin leveraging their retirement and investment accounts to acquire real estate, a new and critical phase emerges—long-term wealth preservation and risk management. While previous chapters focused on gaining access to financing, structuring assets, and building portfolios, this chapter shifts the focus toward protecting what has been built. The true success of asset-based mortgage strategies is not measured solely by approvals or acquisitions, but by the ability to sustain, grow, and protect wealth over time.

One of the most important realities borrowers must accept is that asset-based lending introduces a different type of risk profile compared to traditional income-based borrowing. When income is derived from employment, there is a predictable inflow of cash that supports mortgage payments. In contrast, when income is derived from assets, the sustainability of that income depends on market performance, withdrawal strategies, and long-term planning. This means borrowers must take a more active role in managing their finances to ensure stability.

Market volatility is one of the primary risks associated with asset-based strategies. Retirement and investment accounts are often exposed to fluctuations in stock and bond markets, which can impact the overall value of the portfolio. A significant market downturn can reduce the asset base used for qualification and, more importantly, reduce the financial cushion available to support mortgage payments. Borrowers must plan for these scenarios by maintaining a margin of safety, ensuring that their assets are sufficient even under less favorable conditions.

Diversification is a key tool in managing this risk. A well-diversified portfolio spreads investments across different asset classes, reducing the impact of any single market event. For example, combining equities, fixed income, real estate, and cash reserves can create a more stable financial foundation. While diversification does not eliminate risk, it helps smooth out volatility and provides greater predictability over time. Borrowers who maintain diversified portfolios are better positioned to sustain asset-based income during market fluctuations.

Another critical aspect of wealth preservation is withdrawal strategy. Borrowers using asset depletion or distributions must carefully manage how much they withdraw from their accounts. Excessive withdrawals can deplete assets prematurely, while insufficient withdrawals may limit cash flow and create financial strain. The goal is to establish a sustainable withdrawal rate that balances current needs with long-term preservation. This often involves coordinating with financial advisors and considering factors such as life expectancy, investment returns, and inflation.

Inflation itself is another factor that cannot be ignored. Over time, the cost of living increases, which can erode the purchasing power of both income and assets. Borrowers must ensure that their investment strategies account for inflation, maintaining growth potential that outpaces rising costs. This is particularly important for long-term mortgage obligations, where payments remain fixed while other expenses may increase.

Liquidity management is equally important. While retirement accounts may represent significant wealth, not all of that wealth is immediately accessible. Borrowers must maintain sufficient liquid or near-liquid assets to cover short-term needs, including mortgage payments, maintenance costs, and unexpected expenses. Having a dedicated reserve fund can provide peace of mind and reduce the need to sell investments during unfavorable market conditions. Leverage management is another key component of risk control. While borrowing allows for the acquisition of real estate and the potential for increased returns, excessive leverage can amplify losses and create financial stress. Borrowers must carefully evaluate how much debt they are taking on relative to their asset base, ensuring that they maintain a comfortable margin of safety. This includes considering worst-case scenarios, such as market downturns or unexpected expenses.

Another important consideration is the alignment of real estate and investment strategies. Borrowers should ensure that their property acquisitions and financial portfolios complement each other. For example, rental properties can provide cash flow that offsets mortgage payments, while investment portfolios can provide growth and liquidity. By aligning these elements, borrowers can create a more balanced and resilient financial structure.

Insurance and protection strategies also play a role in wealth preservation. This includes not only property insurance but also broader financial protections such as liability coverage and estate planning. Protecting assets from unforeseen events is an essential part of maintaining long-term stability and ensuring that wealth can be passed on or utilized effectively. As borrowers continue to grow their portfolios, they must also consider succession and legacy planning. Retirement assets, real estate holdings, and other investments should be structured in a way that facilitates smooth انتقال and minimizes complications for heirs. While this extends beyond mortgage qualification, it is an integral part of long-term financial planning.

Another advanced concept is stress testing. Borrowers should periodically evaluate their financial position under different scenarios, such as market declines, interest rate increases, or changes in rental income. By understanding how these factors impact their overall profile, they can make proactive adjustments and avoid reactive decision-making during challenging times.

Behavioral discipline is perhaps one of the most overlooked aspects of wealth preservation. Emotional reactions to market fluctuations, economic news, or personal circumstances can lead to poor financial decisions. Borrowers who maintain a disciplined, long-term perspective are more likely to navigate challenges successfully and preserve their wealth over time.

As borrowers integrate these principles into their overall strategy, they begin to see that asset-based mortgage lending is not just about access—it is about stewardship. It is about managing resources responsibly, making informed decisions, and maintaining control over financial outcomes. This mindset transforms borrowing from a transactional activity into a strategic component of wealth management.

Ultimately, long-term success with asset-based mortgage strategies depends on balance. It requires balancing growth with stability, leverage with caution, and opportunity with discipline. By understanding and applying the principles in this chapter, borrowers can protect their wealth, sustain their investments, and continue to build financial security for years to come.

Real-Life Math Example: Managing Risk and Preserving Wealth Over Time

Consider a borrower named Steven, who is 65 years old and has built a diversified financial portfolio. His assets include $2,000,000 in retirement accounts, $800,000 in a brokerage account, and two rental properties generating a combined $4,000 per month in income. He also has a mortgage on his primary residence with a monthly payment of $3,000.

Steven's total asset base is $2,800,000. After applying a blended discount of approximately 25% to account for taxes and market risk, his usable assets are $2,100,000. Using a 30-year (360-month) asset depletion calculation, this results in a monthly income of approximately $5,833. Adding his rental income (adjusted to $3,000 after vacancy and expenses), Steven's total qualifying income is $8,833 per month. With a mortgage payment of $3,000 and minimal additional debt, his financial position appears strong.

However, Steven wants to ensure that his strategy is sustainable over the long term. He conducts a stress test, assuming a 20% market decline. This reduces his total assets to $2,240,000, and his adjusted usable assets to approximately $1,680,000. Dividing this by 360 months results in a new monthly income of $4,667.

Adding his adjusted rental income of $3,000, his total income becomes $7,667. With a mortgage payment of $3,000, his debt-to-income ratio remains manageable, but his margin of safety has decreased.

To improve his position, Steven implements several risk management strategies. He sets aside $150,000 in a high-liquidity account to cover at least 50 months of mortgage payments. He also adjusts his investment portfolio to include a higher allocation of fixed income assets, reducing overall volatility. Additionally, he uses a portion of his rental income to make extra principal payments on his mortgage, gradually reducing his debt over time.

After these adjustments, Steven's financial profile becomes more resilient. His reduced loan balance lowers his monthly obligations, while his increased liquidity provides a buffer against unexpected events. Even in a downturn scenario, he maintains sufficient income and reserves to sustain his lifestyle and obligations.

This example illustrates how long-term planning, diversification, and disciplined management can preserve wealth and reduce risk in asset-based mortgage strategies. By proactively addressing potential challenges, Steven is able to protect his financial position and continue benefiting from both his investments and real estate holdings.

Chapter 12

Building a Lifetime Strategy with Asset-Based Mortgage Mastery

As you reach the final stage of this series, the focus shifts from individual transactions to the creation of a lifelong financial strategy. Asset-based mortgage lending is not just a tool for qualifying—it is a system that, when used correctly, can support decades of wealth creation, preservation, and flexibility. The true mastery of this approach lies in your ability to integrate everything you have learned into a cohesive plan that evolves with your life, your goals, and the changing economic environment.

At its core, a lifetime strategy built around asset-based mortgage principles is about control. It allows you to move away from dependency on traditional income and instead rely on the strength of your accumulated assets. This shift creates a new level of financial independence, where your ability to acquire property, refinance, or invest is no longer tied to employment status but to the strategic management of your wealth.

The first step in building a lifetime strategy is defining your long-term objectives. These may include owning a primary residence free and clear, building a portfolio of income-producing properties, preserving capital for retirement, or creating a legacy for future generations. Each of these goals requires a different approach to asset allocation, leverage, and risk management. By clearly defining your objectives, you can align your mortgage strategies with your broader financial vision.

One of the most important principles in long-term planning is adaptability. Financial markets, interest rates, and personal circumstances will change over time. A strategy that works today may need to be adjusted in the future. Asset-based mortgage lending provides the flexibility to adapt, allowing you to refinance, restructure, or reposition your assets as conditions evolve. This adaptability is a key advantage over traditional lending models, which are often more rigid and less responsive to change.

Another critical element is the concept of capital efficiency. Rather than allowing assets to sit idle, borrowers can use them strategically to generate returns. For example, instead of paying cash for a property, a borrower may choose to finance it using asset-based qualification, preserving their capital for other investments. This approach allows assets to work in multiple ways simultaneously, increasing overall efficiency and potential returns. Portfolio integration is also essential. Your real estate holdings, retirement accounts, and investment portfolios should not be viewed as separate entities but as interconnected components of a larger system. Decisions in one area will impact the others. For example, using assets for a down payment reduces the base used for asset depletion calculations, while acquiring a rental property may increase income but also introduce new risks. Understanding these interactions allows you to make more informed decisions.

Another advanced concept is strategic refinancing over time. Instead of viewing refinancing as a one-time event, it can be used as an ongoing tool to optimize your financial position. As property values increase and loan balances decrease, refinancing can unlock equity, reduce costs, or reposition debt. When combined with asset-based qualification, this creates a dynamic system where capital can be accessed and redeployed as opportunities arise.

Debt management plays a central role in long-term success. While leverage can enhance returns, it must be used responsibly. Borrowers should aim to maintain a balance between debt and assets, ensuring that they have sufficient reserves and flexibility. Over time, strategic debt reduction—such as making extra principal payments or refinancing into shorter terms—can strengthen the financial foundation and reduce risk. Another key consideration is the role of passive income. Rental properties, dividends, and other income streams can supplement asset-based income, creating a more robust and diversified financial profile. This layered approach reduces reliance on any single source and enhances overall stability. As income streams grow, borrowers may find it easier to qualify for additional opportunities and expand their portfolios.

Tax efficiency continues to be an important factor throughout the lifetime strategy. Decisions about when to withdraw funds, how to structure investments, and how to finance properties can all have tax implications. While this book does not provide tax advice, it emphasizes the importance of coordinating with professionals to ensure that your strategy is optimized from both a lending and tax perspective.

Legacy planning is another critical component. As wealth grows, borrowers must consider how their assets will be transferred and managed in the future. This includes structuring ownership, establishing trusts if appropriate, and ensuring that financial plans align with long-term family goals. Asset-based mortgage strategies can play a role in this process by providing liquidity and flexibility without requiring the liquidation of assets.

Technology and access to information are also transforming how borrowers manage their strategies. Today, borrowers have access to real-time data on property values, investment performance, and market conditions. This allows for more informed decision-making and faster adjustments. Leveraging these tools can enhance your ability to execute and refine your strategy over time.

Behavioral discipline remains one of the most important factors in long-term success. Markets will fluctuate, opportunities will come and go, and external conditions will change. Borrowers who remain focused on their long-term objectives and avoid reactive decision-making are more likely to achieve consistent results. Discipline, patience, and a clear strategy are the foundation of sustainable wealth building.

As you bring all these elements together, you begin to see that asset-based mortgage mastery is not about any single technique—it is about integration. It is about understanding how each component of your financial life interacts with the others and using that knowledge to create a system that works for you. This system should be flexible, resilient, and aligned with your goals.

Ultimately, the journey through this series is about transformation. It is about moving from a traditional mindset—where income dictates opportunity—to a modern approach where assets, strategy, and knowledge define what is possible. By mastering these concepts, you position yourself to take advantage of opportunities, navigate challenges, and build a financial future that is both secure and expansive.

This is not the end of the journey, but the beginning of a new phase—one where you have the tools, understanding, and confidence to operate at a higher level. Your assets are no longer just savings; they are instruments of growth, flexibility, and control. When used wisely, they can support a lifetime of opportunities and create a legacy that extends far beyond any single transaction.

Real-Life Math Example: Designing a Long-Term Asset-Based Mortgage Strategy

Consider a borrower named Angela, who is 50 years old and planning her long-term financial future. Angela has $1,200,000 in retirement accounts, $300,000 in a brokerage account, and $100,000 in cash. She also owns a primary residence with no mortgage and is considering building a portfolio of rental properties over the next 10 to 15 years.

Angela decides to begin by purchasing her first investment property priced at $400,000. She makes a 25% down payment of $100,000, leaving a loan amount of $300,000 with a monthly payment of $2,200. After the down payment, her remaining assets total $1,500,000. The lender evaluates her assets, applying a blended discount of 25%, resulting in usable assets of $1,125,000. Dividing this amount by 360 months produces a monthly income of approximately $3,125. The property is expected to generate $2,000 per month in rent, which is adjusted to $1,500 after applying a vacancy factor.

Angela's total qualifying income is $4,625 per month. With a mortgage payment of $2,200 and minimal additional debt, her debt-to-income ratio is approximately 47.6%, allowing her to qualify for the loan.

Over the next five years, the property appreciates to $500,000, and Angela pays down the loan balance to $260,000. She now has $240,000 in equity. She decides to refinance, accessing $100,000 in equity while securing a similar interest rate. This increases her loan balance but provides capital to acquire a second property.

At the same time, her investment portfolio grows to $1,700,000 due to contributions and market performance. After adjusting for the new loan and additional down payment, her usable assets remain strong, allowing her to qualify for the second property using a similar structure.

As Angela continues this process over time, she builds a portfolio of three to four properties, each generating rental income that supplements her asset-based income. Her combined rental income reaches $6,000 per month, which, after adjustments, contributes $4,500 to her qualifying income.

By the time Angela reaches 65, her portfolio includes multiple properties with significant equity, a strong investment portfolio, and diversified income streams. Her strategy allows her to maintain financial flexibility, generate passive income, and preserve her assets for the future.

This example illustrates how a long-term, integrated approach to asset-based mortgage lending can create a powerful financial system. By combining strategic acquisitions, refinancing, and disciplined asset management, Angela is able to achieve her goals and build a sustainable, scalable financial future.

Chapter 13

Creating a Scalable Asset-Based Mortgage System for Continuous Wealth Expansion

As you move beyond foundational understanding and into true mastery, the next evolution is building a scalable system—one that allows you to repeatedly acquire, refinance, and expand without resetting your financial position each time. This chapter focuses on turning everything you have learned into a repeatable framework that compounds over time. Instead of thinking in terms of individual deals, you begin to think in terms of cycles, systems, and long-term expansion.

A scalable asset-based mortgage system is built on one core principle: preservation of capital while increasing control. Most traditional borrowers deplete their resources each time they purchase property. They use savings for a down payment, rely on income to qualify, and slowly rebuild before attempting the next acquisition. In contrast, an asset-based system is designed to keep your capital working continuously. You are not just spending money—you are positioning it, leveraging it, and redeploying it strategically. The first step in building this system is establishing a strong base layer of assets. This includes retirement accounts, brokerage accounts, and liquid reserves. These assets serve multiple functions simultaneously: they support qualification through asset depletion, provide reserves for lenders, and act as a safety net for risk management. The strength of this base layer determines how aggressively you can scale. The larger and more stable your asset base, the more flexibility you have in structuring deals.

The second layer of the system is your real estate portfolio. Each property you acquire becomes both an asset and a tool. It can generate rental income, appreciate in value, and create equity that can be accessed later. The goal is to build a portfolio where each property contributes to the overall system rather than functioning in isolation. This means selecting properties that align with your strategy—properties that produce consistent cash flow, are located in stable markets, and have strong long-term potential.

One of the most powerful aspects of a scalable system is the ability to recycle capital. Instead of allowing equity to remain locked in a property, you can access it through refinancing or lines of credit and redeploy it into new opportunities. This creates a cycle: acquire, stabilize, refinance, and repeat. Each cycle increases your asset base, expands your portfolio, and strengthens your overall financial position. However, scaling requires careful attention to debt management. As you acquire more properties, your total obligations increase. While asset-based qualification allows you to offset these obligations with your asset base, there are limits. Lenders will evaluate your overall exposure, including debt-to-income ratios, reserves, and asset sustainability. To scale effectively, you must ensure that each new acquisition strengthens your profile rather than weakening it.

Another key element of scalability is efficiency. This includes optimizing how your assets are structured, how your loans are arranged, and how your properties are managed. For example, using similar loan structures across multiple properties can simplify management and improve predictability. Consolidating accounts or maintaining consistent documentation can streamline the underwriting process for future transactions. Efficiency reduces friction, allowing you to move faster and with greater confidence.

Time becomes a critical factor in scaling. Each decision you make today affects your ability to act tomorrow. For example, using too much of your asset base for a single down payment may limit your ability to qualify for the next deal. Conversely, preserving capital and maintaining strong reserves can position you for multiple acquisitions in a shorter period. Understanding this dynamic allows you to pace your growth strategically. Another advanced concept is income layering across a portfolio. As you acquire more properties, rental income becomes an increasingly important component of your qualifying profile. When combined with asset-based income, this creates a powerful dual-income structure. Over time, rental income may even reduce your reliance on asset depletion, allowing your portfolio to become more self-sustaining.

Geographic diversification is also an important consideration in a scalable system. Investing in multiple markets can reduce risk and create additional opportunities. Different regions may offer different advantages, such as higher cash flow, stronger appreciation, or lower entry costs. By diversifying geographically, you can balance these factors and create a more resilient portfolio.

Another key aspect of scaling is adapting to market cycles. Real estate and financial markets move in cycles, and opportunities vary depending on timing. A scalable system allows you to adjust your strategy based on current conditions. In a rising market, you may focus on acquisitions and appreciation. In a stable or declining market, you may prioritize cash flow, refinancing, or debt reduction. Flexibility is essential to long-term success.

Technology and automation can also enhance scalability. Property management systems, financial tracking tools, and data analytics can help you monitor performance, identify opportunities, and make informed decisions. As your portfolio grows, these tools become increasingly valuable, allowing you to manage complexity without becoming overwhelmed.

Another important element is building a team. As you scale, you may benefit from working with real estate agents, property managers, lenders, and financial advisors who understand your strategy. A strong team can provide support, insights, and execution capabilities that enhance your ability to grow. However, it is important to remain actively involved and ensure that all decisions align with your overall plan.

Risk management remains central, even in a growth-focused system. Scaling should not come at the expense of stability. Maintaining reserves, avoiding over-leverage, and regularly reviewing your portfolio are essential practices. A scalable system is not just about growth—it is about sustainable growth.

As you integrate these elements, you begin to operate at a higher level. You are no longer focused on individual transactions but on building a system that generates opportunities continuously. Your assets, properties, and strategies work together, creating momentum and compounding results over time.

Ultimately, a scalable asset-based mortgage system is about creating a financial engine. It is a system that converts assets into opportunities, opportunities into income, and income into further growth. It allows you to expand without starting over, to build without depleting, and to move forward with confidence and control.

Real-Life Math Example: Scaling from One Property to a Multi-Property Portfolio

Consider a borrower named Marcus, who is 52 years old and has $1,500,000 in retirement and investment assets. He begins with no real estate holdings and decides to build a portfolio using an asset-based strategy.

Marcus purchases his first investment property for $300,000, making a 25% down payment of $75,000. This leaves a loan amount of $225,000 with a monthly payment of $1,700. After the down payment, his remaining assets are $1,425,000.

The lender applies a 25% discount to his assets, resulting in usable assets of approximately $1,068,750. Dividing this by 360 months produces a monthly income of about $2,969. The property generates $1,800 in rent, adjusted to $1,350 after a vacancy factor. His total qualifying income is $4,319, and his debt-to-income ratio supports the loan.

After two years, the property appreciates to $350,000, and the loan balance decreases to $215,000. Marcus now has $135,000 in equity. He refinances, accessing $60,000 in cash while maintaining a manageable loan structure.

At the same time, his investment portfolio grows to $1,600,000 due to market performance. After accounting for the refinance and available cash, Marcus uses the $60,000 along with an additional $40,000 from his assets to purchase a second property for $400,000, again with a 25% down payment.

Now Marcus owns two properties. The combined rental income is $3,800 per month, adjusted to $2,850. His asset base, after adjustments, still supports strong qualification. Over time, both properties appreciate, and rental income increases.

Marcus repeats this process over several years. By carefully managing his assets, maintaining reserves, and using refinancing strategically, he acquires a third and fourth property. His portfolio now generates over $7,000 per month in rental income, which significantly supplements his asset-based income.

Even as his asset base fluctuates with market conditions, the growing rental income provides stability. His system becomes increasingly self-sustaining, reducing reliance on asset depletion and allowing him to preserve more of his investment portfolio. This example demonstrates how a scalable system can transform a single acquisition into a growing portfolio. By recycling capital, layering income, and managing risk, Marcus builds a financial engine that continues to expand over time. It highlights the power of combining asset-based qualification with strategic planning to achieve long-term wealth growth.

Chapter 14

Exit Strategies, Liquidity Events, and Converting Assets into Freedom

As you reach the most advanced stage of asset-based mortgage mastery, the focus shifts from acquisition and scaling to strategic exits and liquidity events. While building wealth is essential, the ultimate purpose of any financial system is to create freedom—freedom of time, freedom of choice, and freedom from financial pressure. This chapter explores how to convert accumulated assets, real estate equity, and investment portfolios into usable, flexible capital while preserving long-term stability. It is not about stopping growth, but about transitioning from accumulation to optimization and control.

One of the most important concepts to understand is that an exit is not always about selling everything. In traditional thinking, wealth is often realized through liquidation—selling properties, cashing out investments, and converting everything into cash. While this approach can provide immediate liquidity, it often comes at the cost of taxes, lost future appreciation, and reduced income streams. In asset-based strategies, exits can be structured in more sophisticated ways, allowing you to access liquidity while maintaining ownership and growth potential. Refinancing remains one of the most powerful exit tools. As properties appreciate and loan balances decrease, refinancing allows you to extract equity without selling the asset. This equity can then be used for personal needs, investments, or diversification. Unlike a sale, refinancing does not trigger capital gains taxes, making it a more efficient way to access value. When combined with asset-based qualification, refinancing can be repeated over time, creating multiple liquidity events from a single property.

Another strategy involves partial liquidation. Instead of selling an entire portfolio, borrowers may choose to sell select properties or assets that have reached their peak performance or no longer align with their strategy. This allows for the reallocation of capital into more efficient opportunities or into more stable, income-producing assets. The key is to evaluate each asset individually and determine whether it continues to serve your long-term objectives.

Portfolio rebalancing is closely related to this concept. Over time, certain assets may grow disproportionately, creating concentration risk. By selectively reallocating or restructuring assets, you can maintain a balanced portfolio that aligns with your risk tolerance and financial goals. This may involve shifting from growth-focused investments to income-focused assets, or from higher-risk properties to more stable holdings.

Another advanced exit strategy is transitioning from active to passive income. In the early stages of wealth building, borrowers often take on more active roles—managing properties, making acquisitions, and optimizing structures. As wealth grows, the focus can shift toward simplifying operations and generating consistent, passive income. This may involve hiring property managers, consolidating holdings, or investing in assets that require less direct involvement.

Liquidity events can also be planned around life transitions. Retirement, relocation, or changes in family circumstances may require adjustments to your financial structure. By planning these transitions in advance, you can structure your exits in a way that minimizes disruption and maximizes efficiency. For example, gradually reducing leverage or increasing liquidity in the years leading up to retirement can create a smoother transition.

Another important consideration is tax strategy. While this book does not provide tax advice, it is essential to recognize that different exit strategies have different tax implications. Selling assets may trigger capital gains, while refinancing or borrowing against assets may provide tax advantages. Working with qualified professionals can help you structure your exits in a way that aligns with both your financial and tax objectives. Securities-based strategies also play a role in liquidity planning. Instead of selling investments, borrowers can use them as collateral to access funds. This allows for liquidity without disrupting long-term growth. When used carefully, this approach can provide flexibility and efficiency, particularly for high-net-worth individuals who want to maintain their investment positions.

Another advanced concept is creating a "cash flow cushion." This involves building a portfolio of assets that generate consistent income, sufficient to cover living expenses and financial obligations. Once this threshold is reached, borrowers can reduce reliance on active income or asset depletion, creating a stable financial foundation. This is often the point where true financial independence begins to take shape.

Debt strategy also evolves during the exit phase. While leverage is useful during growth, reducing or restructuring debt can improve stability and reduce risk. This may involve paying down loans, refinancing into more favorable terms, or consolidating obligations. The goal is to create a balance where debt supports your strategy without creating unnecessary pressure.

Another important element is legacy and wealth transfer. As you approach the later stages of your financial journey, you may begin to consider how your assets will be passed on or utilized by future generations. Structuring your portfolio in a way that facilitates smooth transitions and preserves value is an essential part of long-term planning.

Emotional and psychological factors also come into play during this phase. Letting go of assets, even strategically, can be challenging. Borrowers must balance the desire for growth with the need for stability and simplicity. Understanding your personal goals and priorities is critical in making these decisions.

As you integrate these strategies, you begin to see that exits are not endpoints—they are transitions. They represent a shift from one phase of your financial journey to another. When executed correctly, they enhance your flexibility, increase your control, and bring you closer to financial freedom.

Ultimately, the purpose of asset-based mortgage mastery is not just to build wealth, but to use that wealth in a way that supports your life. Whether that means reducing obligations, increasing income, or creating more time and flexibility, the strategies in this chapter provide a framework for achieving those outcomes.

Real-Life Math Example: Transitioning from Growth to Financial Freedom

Consider a borrower named Laura, who is 62 years old and has built a substantial portfolio over the past 15 years. She owns four investment properties with a combined value of $1,800,000 and total loan balances of $800,000. Her properties generate $9,000 per month in rental income, which is adjusted to $6,750 after expenses and vacancy.

In addition to her real estate holdings, Laura has $2,000,000 in retirement and investment accounts. Her total net worth is approximately $3,000,000. She wants to transition into a more passive lifestyle, reduce her involvement in property management, and ensure that her income is stable and sufficient for her needs.

Laura begins by evaluating her portfolio. She identifies one property that has appreciated significantly but produces relatively low cash flow. The property is valued at $600,000 with a remaining loan balance of $200,000. She decides to sell this property, generating $400,000 in equity before taxes.

She uses a portion of these proceeds to pay down $200,000 in debt across her remaining properties, reducing her total loan balance to $600,000. This lowers her monthly obligations and improves her overall financial stability. The remaining

$200,000 is invested into income-producing assets, generating approximately $1,000 per month.

Her remaining properties now generate $7,000 per month in rental income, adjusted to $5,250. Combined with her investment income of $1,000, her total monthly income is $6,250. Additionally, her reduced debt lowers her financial obligations, increasing her net cash flow.

Laura also refinances one of her properties to secure a lower interest rate, further reducing her monthly payments. This combination of actions—selling a low-performing asset, reducing debt, and increasing passive income—transforms her financial profile.

She now has fewer properties to manage, lower debt, and a more stable income stream. Her retirement and investment accounts remain intact, continuing to grow and provide additional security.

This example demonstrates how strategic exits and liquidity events can be used to transition from active growth to financial freedom. By carefully evaluating her assets and making targeted adjustments, Laura is able to simplify her portfolio, reduce risk, and create a sustainable, passive income structure that supports her lifestyle.

Chapter 15

Building a Legacy and Creating Generational Wealth Through Asset-Based Mortgage Strategies

As you arrive at the final chapter of this extended series, the conversation expands beyond personal wealth and financial independence into something even more meaningful—legacy. The true power of asset-based mortgage strategies is not only in what they can create for you during your lifetime, but in what they can establish for future generations. When structured correctly, the combination of real estate, retirement assets, and strategic financing can become a self-sustaining system that continues to provide income, stability, and opportunity long after you are no longer actively managing it.

Legacy building begins with a shift in perspective. Instead of focusing solely on accumulation, you begin to think in terms of continuity. How will your assets function without you? How can your financial system continue to generate income and preserve value for your family? These questions require intentional planning, disciplined execution, and a clear understanding of how each component of your financial structure interacts with the others. One of the most powerful aspects of asset-based mortgage strategies in legacy planning is the ability to retain ownership while still accessing liquidity. Unlike traditional approaches that rely heavily on liquidation, asset-based strategies allow you to maintain control of appreciating assets such as real estate and investment portfolios. This means that your heirs can benefit not only from the current value of these assets but also from their future growth and income potential.

Real estate plays a central role in generational wealth because of its unique combination of appreciation, income, and leverage. A well-structured portfolio of properties can provide consistent cash flow, hedge against inflation, and increase in value over time. When these properties are financed strategically, they can be acquired and expanded without depleting existing assets, creating a compounding effect that strengthens the overall portfolio.

Retirement and investment accounts complement this structure by providing liquidity, diversification, and long-term growth. These accounts can support mortgage qualification, serve as reserves, and act as a financial buffer during market fluctuations. When integrated with real estate holdings, they create a balanced system that combines stability with opportunity. Another key element of legacy building is simplification. While complex structures may be effective during the growth phase, they can become burdensome for future generations if not properly organized. Streamlining accounts, standardizing loan structures, and clearly documenting financial strategies can make it easier for heirs to understand and manage the system. The goal is to create a structure that is both effective and accessible.

Education is equally important. Passing down assets without passing down knowledge can lead to mismanagement and loss of value. By educating your family about how your financial system works—how properties are financed, how assets are structured, and how decisions are made—you empower them to continue and build upon what you have created. This knowledge becomes an intangible asset that is just as valuable as the financial resources themselves.

Another important consideration is income continuity. A strong legacy system should provide ongoing income that supports future generations. This can come from rental properties, dividends, interest, or other passive income streams. By ensuring that your assets generate consistent cash flow, you create a foundation that can support financial stability and independence for years to come.

Debt strategy also plays a role in legacy planning. While leverage is useful for growth, excessive or poorly structured debt can create challenges for heirs. As part of a long-term strategy, borrowers may choose to reduce or restructure debt over time, ensuring that the portfolio remains manageable and sustainable. In some cases, maintaining low-interest, long-term debt can be advantageous, particularly if the assets generate sufficient income to cover the obligations.

Another advanced concept is asset protection. Protecting your wealth from unforeseen risks—such as market downturns, legal issues, or economic changes—is essential to preserving your legacy. This includes maintaining diversification, adequate insurance, and a conservative approach to leverage. A well-protected portfolio is more likely to withstand challenges and continue providing value over time.

Liquidity planning is also critical. While long-term assets like real estate are valuable, they are not always easily converted into cash. Ensuring that your financial system includes sufficient liquid assets allows for flexibility and reduces the need for forced sales. This is particularly important during transitions, such as generational transfers or unexpected events.

Another important aspect of legacy building is alignment with personal values. Wealth is not just about numbers—it is about purpose. Whether your goal is to provide security for your family, support education, or create opportunities for future generations, your financial strategy should reflect these priorities. This alignment ensures that your legacy is not only financially successful but also meaningful.

As you move into this phase, you begin to see that asset-based mortgage strategies are not just tools for growth—they are tools for continuity. They allow you to create a system that extends beyond your own lifetime, providing benefits that can be felt for generations. This perspective transforms the way you approach every decision, from acquisitions to refinancing to asset allocation.

Another key element is adaptability across generations. Future market conditions, technologies, and financial systems may differ from those of today. By building a flexible and resilient structure, you ensure that your legacy can evolve and remain relevant. This includes maintaining diversified assets, avoiding overly rigid structures, and fostering a mindset of continuous learning.

Ultimately, building generational wealth through asset-based mortgage strategies is about creating a living system—one that grows, adapts, and continues to provide value over time. It is about combining financial knowledge with intentional planning, ensuring that your efforts today create opportunities for tomorrow.

Real-Life Math Example: Creating a Multi-Generational Income System

Consider a borrower named Richard, who is 60 years old and has spent the past two decades building a diversified financial portfolio. His assets include $2,500,000 in retirement and investment accounts and five rental properties with a combined value of $2,500,000 and total loan balances of $1,000,000.

Richard's properties generate $12,000 per month in rental income. After accounting for expenses and vacancy, the adjusted income is $9,000 per month. His total monthly mortgage payments across all properties are $5,000, resulting in a net cash flow of $4,000 per month.

His investment portfolio, conservatively estimated to generate a 5% annual return, produces approximately $125,000 per year, or about $10,400 per month in growth and income. Combined with his rental income, Richard's total monthly financial benefit exceeds $14,000.

As Richard approaches retirement, he begins to restructure his portfolio with a focus on legacy. He pays down $300,000 in debt using a portion of his investment accounts, reducing his total loan balance to $700,000 and lowering his monthly mortgage payments to $3,500. This increases his net rental cash flow to $5,500 per month. He also consolidates his properties under a simplified management structure, making it easier for his family to oversee operations. His remaining investment portfolio continues to grow, providing additional security and flexibility.

Richard's total monthly income now includes $5,500 from real estate and approximately $10,000 from his investment portfolio, creating a combined income of $15,500. This income exceeds his personal needs, allowing him to reinvest surplus funds or allocate them toward family goals.

Over time, as properties appreciate and loans are paid down further, the equity in his real estate portfolio increases significantly. His heirs inherit a system that includes income-producing properties, a strong investment portfolio, and a clear structure for management and growth.

This example illustrates how asset-based mortgage strategies can be used to create a lasting financial legacy. By combining real estate, investments, and strategic debt management, Richard builds a system that not only supports his own lifestyle but also provides ongoing benefits for future generations. It demonstrates the power of long-term thinking, disciplined execution, and the integration of multiple financial strategies into a cohesive, sustainable plan.

Final Thoughts

Mastering the Future of Asset-Based Mortgage Lending

As you reach the conclusion of this series, it is important to recognize that what you have learned is far more than a collection of mortgage strategies—it is a complete shift in how you think about money, qualification, and financial opportunity. Traditional lending systems have long conditioned borrowers to believe that income is the primary driver of access. You were taught that your paycheck determines your potential, that your job defines your borrowing power, and that your financial future is limited by how much you earn each month. This series has challenged that belief and replaced it with a more powerful truth: your assets, your strategy, and your understanding of financial systems are what truly determine your ability to move forward.

Asset-based mortgage lending is not a shortcut or a loophole. It is a legitimate, structured, and increasingly important evolution in the world of finance. It reflects a broader shift in how wealth is created and managed in today's economy. More people are stepping away from traditional employment models and building wealth through investments, businesses, and long-term financial planning. As this trend continues, the need for flexible, asset-driven lending solutions will only grow. By understanding these principles now, you are positioning yourself ahead of the curve, equipped with knowledge that most borrowers—and even many professionals—do not yet fully grasp.

One of the most important takeaways from this journey is that financial strength is not defined by income alone. A borrower with substantial assets, disciplined management, and a clear strategy can often be in a stronger position than someone with a high salary but limited savings or poor financial habits. This realization opens the door to a new way of thinking, where the focus shifts from earning more to managing and leveraging what you already have. It is a mindset that prioritizes efficiency, control, and long-term sustainability.

Throughout this series, you have seen how retirement accounts, investment portfolios, and real estate equity can be transformed into powerful tools for qualification. You have learned how lenders evaluate these assets, how to structure them effectively, and how to combine them with other income sources to create a strong financial profile. More importantly, you have learned how to think like an underwriter—how to anticipate questions, address potential concerns, and present your financial story in a way that aligns with lender expectations. This skill alone can dramatically improve your ability to navigate the mortgage process. You have also explored how these strategies extend beyond a single transaction. Asset-based mortgage lending is not just about buying a home—it is about building a system. It is about creating a framework where your assets work together to support your goals, whether that involves acquiring properties, refinancing to access equity, or preserving wealth for the future. This system is dynamic, adaptable, and capable of evolving with your life. It allows you to respond to opportunities and challenges with confidence, rather than being constrained by rigid financial structures.

Another key lesson is the importance of balance. While asset-based strategies provide powerful opportunities, they also require discipline and responsibility. Leverage must be used carefully, assets must be managed thoughtfully, and risks must be understood and mitigated. The goal is not to maximize borrowing at all costs, but to create a sustainable financial structure that supports long-term success. This means maintaining reserves, diversifying investments, and avoiding decisions that compromise stability in pursuit of short-term gains.

Risk management has been a recurring theme throughout this series, and for good reason. Markets fluctuate, interest rates change, and unexpected events can occur at any time. Borrowers who rely on assets rather than income must be especially mindful of these factors, as their financial stability is closely tied to the performance and accessibility of those assets. By planning for different scenarios, maintaining liquidity, and adopting a disciplined approach, you can navigate these uncertainties and protect your financial position.

As you move forward, it is also important to recognize the role of professional guidance. While this series provides a comprehensive framework, the implementation of these strategies often involves coordination with mortgage professionals, financial advisors, and other experts. Working with individuals who understand asset-based lending can enhance your results, providing insights, options, and support that align with your goals. At the same time, your own understanding remains your greatest asset, allowing you to ask the right questions and make informed decisions.

One of the most empowering aspects of this approach is the flexibility it provides. You are no longer tied to a single path or dependent on a single source of income. You have the ability to structure your finances in a way that aligns with your lifestyle, your ambitions, and your vision for the future. Whether you choose to focus on real estate, investments, or a combination of both, asset-based mortgage strategies give you the tools to move forward on your own terms. This flexibility also extends to timing. In traditional lending, opportunities are often dictated by employment status or income documentation. In the asset-based world, you can act when the market presents an opportunity, using your assets to support your decisions. This can be a significant advantage in competitive environments, where speed and certainty are critical. By being prepared and strategically positioned, you can capitalize on opportunities that others may miss.

As you reflect on everything you have learned, consider how these principles apply to your own situation. Every borrower's financial profile is unique, and there is no one-size-fits-all approach. The key is to take the concepts you have learned and adapt them to your specific goals and circumstances. This may involve restructuring your assets, adjusting your investment strategy, or exploring new opportunities that align with your long-term vision.

It is also important to think about the future. The financial landscape will continue to evolve, and new opportunities and challenges will emerge. By staying informed, remaining adaptable, and continuing to refine your strategy, you can ensure that you remain in a position of strength. Asset-based mortgage mastery is not a destination—it is an ongoing process of learning, adjusting, and improving.

At its highest level, this approach is about empowerment. It is about taking control of your financial life and using your resources in a way that supports your goals. It is about moving beyond limitations and creating opportunities where none seemed to exist. It is about understanding that your assets are not just numbers on a statement, but tools that can be used to build a better future.

As you close this chapter, remember that the knowledge you have gained is only valuable if it is applied. Take the time to evaluate your current financial position, identify opportunities for improvement, and begin implementing the strategies that resonate with you. Start with small, intentional steps, and build momentum over time. Each decision you make brings you closer to a more flexible, resilient, and empowered financial future.

The world of asset-based mortgage lending is still evolving, and those who understand it today are in a unique position to benefit. By embracing these strategies, you are not just adapting to change—you are leading it. You are redefining what it means to qualify, to invest, and to build wealth in a modern economy.

Your journey does not end here. In many ways, it is just beginning. Armed with knowledge, strategy, and a new perspective, you now have the ability to shape your financial future with intention and confidence. The path ahead is yours to design, and the tools you need are already within your reach.

How to Get a Personalized Asset-Based Mortgage Review

Asset-based lending is highly customized—your assets, liquidity, credit profile, property type, and long-term goals all play a role in determining what you qualify for and how your loan should be structured.

Every borrower's situation is different. The type of assets you hold, how those assets are allocated, your credit history, the property you are purchasing or refinancing, and current lender guidelines all affect your options. The strategies and examples in this book are designed to teach you how asset-based mortgage loans work—but your actual qualifying income, loan amount, and structure can only be determined by reviewing your real numbers.

If you would like a no-obligation Asset-Based Mortgage review, you can request one here:

Email: **info@FinibiMortgage.com**

A licensed mortgage broker will review your assets, credit profile, and goals, and explain what asset-based mortgage options may be available to you—including asset depletion loans, investment property financing, refinancing strategies, and advanced structuring approaches tailored to your situation.

No cost. No pressure. No obligation.

Sincerely,

Joseph G. Correa

Finibi Mortgage Inc.

Licensed Mortgage Broker

About the Author

Joseph G. Correa is a licensed mortgage broker and the founder of Finibi Mortgage, a Florida-based brokerage specializing in asset-based mortgage lending, alternative financing, and strategic real estate funding solutions for homeowners, investors, and high-net-worth borrowers. With more than two decades of experience in mortgage lending, underwriting, and financial structuring, Joseph has helped thousands of clients qualify for real estate using assets instead of traditional income, unlocking opportunities that conventional lending often restricts.

Unlike traditional loan officers who focus solely on income-based approvals, Joseph's approach is centered on asset positioning, financial strategy, and long-term wealth building. He believes that mortgages should not be limited by outdated income rules, but instead structured around true financial strength—assets, liquidity, and intelligent leverage. This philosophy has made him a trusted advisor for entrepreneurs, retirees, self-employed individuals, and investors who need flexible financing solutions that align with how they actually build and manage wealth.

Joseph is widely recognized for his expertise in asset depletion mortgage loans, bank statement programs, non-QM lending, investment property financing, and advanced structuring strategies that allow borrowers to qualify without relying on tax returns or W-2 income. His ability to simplify complex underwriting guidelines into clear, actionable strategies has helped clients use their savings, investment portfolios, and retirement accounts to acquire real estate, scale portfolios, and preserve liquidity.

Through his education platform, Finibi Academy, Joseph has trained tens of thousands of students worldwide in mortgage strategy, credit optimization, real estate investing, and financial independence. His courses and books are designed for both beginners and experienced professionals who want a deeper understanding of how modern lending truly works beyond traditional income-based limitations.

Joseph created The Asset-Based Mortgage Mastery Series to provide a clear, practical roadmap for borrowers and professionals who want to leverage assets instead of income to qualify for real estate. His mission is simple: to help people understand how to use their assets as a powerful financial tool, eliminate unnecessary barriers to financing, and build long-term wealth through strategic lending.

When he is not structuring loans or writing, Joseph works with clients across the United States to design customized asset-based mortgage strategies that align with their financial goals, liquidity needs, and long-term investment plans.

The Asset-Based Mortgage Mastery Series Roadmap

The Professional Guide to Qualifying for Real Estate Using Assets, Not Income

The purpose of *The Asset-Based Mortgage Mastery Series* is to give borrowers, investors, and financial professionals the same strategies used by banks, private lenders, and institutional investors—translated into clear, practical guidance that can be applied in real life. This series is designed to take you from foundational understanding to advanced mastery of how to qualify for, structure, and scale real estate financing using assets instead of traditional income.

Each book builds on the last. You are not just learning how to get approved—you are learning how to think, structure, and operate like the institutions that control capital.

Book 1 — Asset-Based Mortgage Loan Fundamentals

This book gives you the foundation. You will understand how asset-based mortgage loans work, how asset depletion is calculated, how lenders evaluate risk, and why income is no longer the only path to qualification. This is where you shift your mindset from income-based borrowing to asset-based strategy.

Book 2 — Retirement Asset Mortgage Qualification

This book focuses on using retirement accounts such as

401(k)s, IRAs, and investment portfolios to qualify for mortgage loans. You will learn how lenders evaluate retirement assets, how to access them strategically, and how to structure your finances to qualify without disrupting long-term retirement growth.

Book 3 — High-Net-Worth Asset-Based Mortgage Strategies

This book is designed for borrowers with significant assets who want to optimize leverage, preserve liquidity, and structure large or complex transactions. You will learn how wealthy borrowers qualify without traditional income and how to position assets for maximum efficiency and control.

Book 4 — Primary Residence Asset-Based Mortgage Loans

This book shows you how to purchase or refinance your primary home using assets instead of income. You will learn how to structure down payments, reserves, and loan options to maximize flexibility while maintaining long-term financial stability.

Book 5 — Investment Property Asset-Based Mortgage Loans This book focuses on building a real estate portfolio using asset-based lending. You will learn how to qualify for multiple properties, integrate rental income, manage reserves, and scale your investments without being limited by income.

Book 6 — Securities-Based Mortgage Lending Strategies

This book explores how to use stocks, bonds, and brokerage accounts to secure financing. You will learn how to leverage investment portfolios without liquidating them, preserving growth while accessing capital for real estate opportunities.

Book 7 — Foreign National Asset-Based Mortgage Loans

This book explains how international buyers can qualify for U.S. real estate using global assets. You will learn how lenders evaluate foreign income and assets, and how to structure deals across borders with confidence.

Book 8 — Jumbo Asset-Based Mortgage Loans

This book focuses on financing high-value and luxury properties. You will learn how to structure large loan amounts, meet stricter guidelines, and position assets to qualify for jumbo financing without traditional income.

Book 9 — Asset-Based Mortgage Refinancing & Equity Access

This book teaches you how to unlock equity from existing properties using asset-based strategies. You will learn how to refinance without income, access liquidity, and use your equity to fund new investments or opportunities.

Book 10 — Advanced Asset-Based Mortgage Structuring

This book brings everything together. You will learn how to engineer approvals, layer assets, sequence transactions, and create sophisticated financing strategies that maximize flexibility, control, and long-term growth.

This series is designed to move you step-by-step from understanding to execution to mastery. By the end, you will not just know how to qualify for loans—you will understand how to control capital, structure wealth, and build a financial system that works for you long-term.

Educational & Financial Disclaimer

The *Asset-Based Mortgage Mastery Series* is intended for educational and informational purposes only. The content provided throughout this series is designed to help readers better understand asset-based mortgage lending, real estate financing strategies, and financial structuring concepts. It is not intended to be, and should not be interpreted as, financial, legal, tax, investment, or mortgage advice.

Joseph G. Correa and Live Stronger Faster are not acting as your personal financial advisor, attorney, accountant, or licensed mortgage professional in any jurisdiction through this publication. All information is presented in a general format and may not apply to your specific financial situation, goals, or circumstances. Readers are strongly encouraged to consult with qualified professionals—including licensed mortgage brokers, financial advisors, tax professionals, and attorneys—before making any financial or real estate decisions.

Mortgage lending guidelines, underwriting standards, and loan program availability vary by lender, location, and over time. Asset-based mortgage programs, including asset depletion loans and non-qualified mortgage (Non-QM) products, are subject to change without notice. The examples, strategies, and scenarios presented in this series are for illustration purposes only and do not guarantee approval, specific loan terms, or financial outcomes. Individual results will vary based on credit profile, asset structure, property type, market conditions, and lender requirements.

Real estate investing and the use of leverage involve risk. Property values can fluctuate, interest rates can change, and market conditions may impact both income and asset performance. While asset-based lending provides flexibility, it also requires careful planning, risk management, and financial discipline. Readers are responsible for evaluating their own risk tolerance and making decisions that align with their long-term financial goals.

Any references to potential income, returns, cash flow, or financial growth are not guarantees or promises of performance. These outcomes depend on multiple factors beyond the control of the author and publisher, including economic conditions, market trends, borrower decisions, and lender policies.

The author and publisher make no representations or warranties regarding the accuracy, completeness, or reliability of the information contained in this series. While every effort has been made to provide accurate and up-to-date information, errors or omissions may occur. The author and publisher disclaim any liability for losses, damages, or consequences resulting from the use or misuse of the information provided.

By reading this series, you acknowledge that you are solely responsible for your financial decisions and actions. The purpose of this content is to provide knowledge, perspective, and strategic insight—not to replace professional advice or guarantee specific outcomes.

Use this information as a guide, not a substitute for professional consultation, and always make decisions based on your individual financial situation, goals, and risk tolerance.

Risk Disclosure

The *Asset-Based Mortgage Mastery Series* discusses financial strategies involving real estate, lending, leverage, and asset-based qualification methods. These strategies involve inherent risks, and it is important that all readers fully understand and accept these risks before applying any concepts presented in this series.

Real estate markets are subject to fluctuation. Property values may rise or fall due to economic conditions, interest rate changes, local market dynamics, or unforeseen events. There is no guarantee that any property will appreciate in value or generate consistent income. Investments in real estate may result in financial loss.

The use of leverage, including mortgage financing and asset-based lending, increases both potential returns and potential risks. Borrowing against assets or property can amplify losses if market conditions change or if income from investments does not perform as expected. Failure to meet loan obligations may result in foreclosure, loss of property, or damage to credit.

Asset-based mortgage lending relies on the valuation and accessibility of financial assets. Investment accounts, retirement funds, and other assets may fluctuate in value due to market volatility. A decline in asset value may impact a borrower's financial position, liquidity, and ability to refinance or secure additional financing.

Interest rates may change over time, particularly with adjustable-rate or interest-only loan structures. Rising interest rates can increase monthly payments, reduce cash flow, and affect long-term affordability. Borrowers must be prepared for potential payment increases and plan accordingly.

Liquidity risk is another important consideration. While asset-based lending allows borrowers to qualify using assets, those assets may be tied up in investments or subject to penalties or restrictions. In times of financial stress, accessing funds may not be as immediate or favorable as expected.

Rental income and investment returns are not guaranteed. Vacancy, tenant issues, maintenance costs, property management expenses, and market conditions can all impact cash flow. Relying on projected income without accounting for these variables can create financial strain.

Refinancing and equity access strategies depend on market conditions, property values, and lender guidelines. There is no assurance that refinancing will be available in the future or that favorable terms will be offered. Changes in lending standards or economic conditions may limit access to capital.

Private lending, capital recycling, and advanced financial strategies discussed in this series involve additional layers of risk, including borrower default, insufficient collateral, and market uncertainty. These strategies require careful due diligence and risk management.

Tax laws and regulations may change over time, affecting the benefits of certain strategies such as depreciation, capital gains deferral, or asset structuring. Readers should consult with qualified tax professionals to understand how these changes may impact their financial plans.

All financial decisions involve risk, and past performance or examples presented in this series do not guarantee future results. The scenarios and illustrations provided are for educational purposes only and may not reflect actual outcomes. Individual results will vary based on personal circumstances, market conditions, and execution.

By using the information in this series, you acknowledge that you understand the risks involved and accept full responsibility for your financial decisions. The author and publisher are not liable for any losses, damages, or outcomes resulting from the application of the concepts discussed.

It is essential to approach asset-based lending and real estate investing with careful planning, professional guidance, and a clear understanding of your financial goals and risk tolerance.

www.ingramcontent.com/pod-product-compliance
Lightning Source LLC
LaVergne TN
LVHW022224200926
848481LV00006B/2103
9798295795275